The Fantasy of Feminist History

Next Wave Provocations

A series edited by Inderpal Grewal, Caren Kaplan, and Robyn Wiegman

A JOHN HOPE FRANKLIN CENTER BOOK

JOAN WALLACH SCOTT

The Fantasy of Feminist History

Duke University Press

DURHAM AND LONDON   2011

© 2011 Duke University Press

All rights reserved

Printed in the United States of America

on acid-free paper ∞

Designed by C. H. Westmoreland

Typeset in Arno Pro by Keystone Typesetting, Inc.

Library of Congress Cataloging-in-Publication Data

appear on the last printed page of this book.

Chapter 1, "Feminism's History," was originally
published in the *Journal of Women's History*, 16, no. 2:
(2004), © 2004 *Journal of Women's History*.

Chapter 2, "Fantasy Echo," originally appeared in
Critical Inquiry 27 (Winter 2001), © 2001 by the
University of Chicago.

Chapter 3, "Femininist Reverberations," originally
appeared in *differences* 13 (Fall 2002), © 2003 by
Brown University and *differences*.

Contents

Acknowledgments

For their critical input into these essays I wish to thank Andrew Aisenberg, Wendy Brown, Judith Butler, Gil Chaitin, Brian Connolly, Eric Fassin, Françoise Gaspard, Ben Kafka, Saba Mahmood, Miglena Nikolchina, Claude Servan-Schreiber, Judith Surkis, and Elizabeth Weed. I am also grateful to the anonymous readers for Duke University Press and to Ken Wissoker, who sent me back to the drawing board more than once in an effort to get the book right. As usual, Nancy Cotterman's patient, careful attention to the details of the manuscript, Donne Petito's gracious willingness to help out, and Laura McCune's able assistance made my work not only easier but better. The library staff at the Institute for Advanced Study, particularly Marcia Tucker, provided invaluable support for which I am grateful. This book is dedicated to Denise Riley, whose intellectual creativity has long enriched my thinking and whose friendship enriches my life.

Introduction:
"Flyers into the Unknown"
Gender, History, and Psychoanalysis

> This tendency on the part of historians to become buried in their own conservatism strikes me as truly regrettable. . . . If progress is to be made we must certainly have new ideas, new points of view, and new techniques. We must be ready, from time to time, to take flyers into the unknown, even though some of them may prove wide of the mark.
> —WILLIAM L. LANGER, "The Next Assignment"

> That is why we must do justice to Freud.
> —MICHEL FOUCAULT, *Madness and Civilization*

I've never forgotten the review of my first book, *The Glassworkers of Carmaux* (1974), by Professor Harold Parker, a historian at Duke University. What stayed with me wasn't the abundant praise he offered (the title of the review was "A Methodological Gem")—though I surely appreciated that—it was instead his one critical remark ("Is this gem without flaw?"). This had to do with the fact that the book, "despite the revealing personal incidents about obscure worker personalities, is too coldly analytical." He went on:

> Scott herself is a very warm person, but there is too little passion, too little madness in her work. Man is precariously sane, in the sense that his images of himself, of other people, and of the universe are rarely correct. Sometimes, when passion enters, his images are completely off. The scientific enterprise, in history as well as in other subjects, is dedicated to the endeavor to make the images correspond to visual and analytical reality. But part of the reality is that men are often mad, and the historian has to show that. In her next book, I am sure Scott will.[1]

It took me a long time—more than thirty years—to appreciate the wisdom offered by this historian of the Napoleonic era.[2] After that review I produced several more books, none of which fully accepted his suggestion about the need to attend to passion and madness in the writing of history. My interest in psychoanalysis—theorizing the reality of that madness—came late, and after much resistance. Among other objections, I found the uses that some psycho-historians made of Freudian concepts reductive and unhelpful, an application of diagnostic classifications to behavior that, even when labeled, remained puzzling. Michel de Certeau has said of their approach that "they circumscribe what cannot be explained, but they do not explain it."[3] I also thought that history, with its insistence on specificity, variability, and change, was incompatible with psychoanalysis, which dealt with individual pathologies and, when it came to gender, universalized the categories and the relationships of women and men, fixing the sexes in permanent antagonism.[4] There was a normative side to this that I resisted, too, as I took descriptions of the psychic operations of sexual difference to be prescriptions for their regulation. Beyond that, though, I now think I considered the study of sex and sexuality—at the center, after all, of psychoanalytic theorizing—somehow trivial in comparison to the large social and economic forces that shape human action. I operated within a more or less binary conceptual framework in which sex was on the side of the private (even if I could recite my feminist lesson that the personal was political), while forces and structures were the public side that provided historians with their explanations.

My early work in women's history took this approach, and even when I began writing about gender, it was as a social category that had little to do with unconscious processes, what Professor Parker deemed "passion" and "madness." Fascination with the workings of language (by way of Derrida, Foucault, and feminist literary criticism) led me slowly to Freud and Lacan and feminist psychoanalytic theorists.[5] It took time for me to see the connections between psychoanalysis and the poststructuralist interrogations of foundational concepts and categories that increasingly drew my attention; to grasp that reading for rupture and contradiction was what Freudian analysis was about; to understand that the point was not to close a case by applying a label to it, but to open things up by exploring the ambiguous meanings that were attached to intractable problems and unanswerable questions. Reading Certeau, a student of history, religion, and Lacanian psychoanalysis, helped articulate some of this for me. I find his critique of history's disciplinary assumptions compelling:

> To be sure, historiography is "familiar" with the question of the other, dealing especially with the relation which the present holds with the past. But its discipline must create proper places for each, by pigeonholing the past into an area other than the present, or else by supposing a continuity of genealogical filiation (by way of a homeland, a nation, a milieu, etc. . . .). Technically, it endlessly presupposes homogeneous unities (century, country, class, economic or social strata, etc.) and cannot give way to the vertigo that critical examination of these fragile boundaries might bring about: historiography does not want to know this. In all of its labors, based on these classifications, historiography takes it for granted that the place where it is itself produced has the capacity to provide meaning, since the current institutional demarcations of the discipline uphold the divisions of time and space in the last resort. In this respect, historical discourse, which is political in essence, takes the *law of place* for granted. It legitimizes a place, that of its production, by "including" others in a relation of filiation or of exteriority.[6]

Certeau thought this kind of thinking could be shaken by an encounter with psychoanalysis, by attention to the psychic investments historians had in the stories they produced, as well as to those of the subjects about whom they wrote. The beneficial "vertigo" produced by "critical examination" would expose the conflicts and contradictions contained by categories presumed to be homogeneous, challenge the entirely rational explanations usually given for human action, and make historians more aware of their own investments in writing about the past.

Certeau's idea of interdisciplinarity—in this instance, the bringing together of history and psychoanalysis—rejected the importation of concepts "transformed into figures of style,"[7] calling instead for confrontation and differentiation: "The interdisciplinarity we look toward would attempt to apprehend epistemological constellations as they reciprocally provide themselves with a new delimitation of their objects and a new status for their procedures."[8] I take this to mean precisely that vertiginous "critical examination of . . . fragile boundaries" and of the work they do in maintaining disciplinary blind spots. For Certeau, psychoanalysis enables a critique of historical practice and, beyond that, the writing of a different kind of history. This has more to do with methods of reading and interpreting than it does with categorizing and classifying. Like Freudian praxis, he suggests, it could "locate its veritable meaning not in the elucidation with which it replaces former representation, but in the ever-unfinished *act* of elucidation."[9] Ambiguous words would be read for what their ambiguity revealed, not for given settled meanings; and there would always be surprises—not just in the form of unexpected documents in a box of archival materials, but in the words chosen to express ideas, in the form and content of representations, in slips of the tongue and the pen, in parenthetical remarks aimed at containing some irrepressible, mad thought.

The essays collected in this book represent my engagement with psychoanalytic theory as a critical reading practice for history. They are particularly concerned with women's history and gender, a concept I have long championed as useful for thinking about the historical constitution of relationships between women and men, the articulation in different contexts (including cultural and temporal) of meanings for sex and sexual difference. I have never been entirely satisfied with my own formulations, and I am positively distressed at the way in which gender has so often been emptied of its most radical implications, treated as a known referent instead of a way to get at meanings that are neither literal nor transparent. So, I've looked for ways to more forcefully insist on its mutability. I'm sure that some readers find it ironic that psychoanalysis is what permits that historicization. But it's not the psychoanalysis associated with normative prescription, not the psychoanalysis invoked to pathologize homosexuality, not the psychoanalysis that assigns individuals to categories. It's the theory that posits sexual difference as an unresolvable dilemma.[10]

When understood this way, I argue, psychoanalysis animates the concept of gender for historians. Gender is no longer simply a social construction, a way of organizing social, economic, and political divisions of labor along sexually differentiated lines. It is instead a historically and culturally specific attempt to resolve the dilemma of sexual difference, to assign fixed meaning to that which ultimately cannot be fixed. Sexual differences are defined neither as a transcendent male/female opposition, nor simply as man's wholeness and woman's lack, but as an intractable problem that defies single solutions. It is precisely the futile struggle to hold meaning in place that makes gender such an interesting historical object, one that includes not only regimes of truth about sex and sexuality, but also the fantasies and transgressions that refuse to be regulated or categorized. Indeed it is fantasy that undermines any notion of psychic immutability or fixed identity, that infuses rational motives with unquenchable desire, that contributes to the actions and events we narrate as history. From this perspective, fantasy becomes a critically useful tool for historical analysis, as I argue in chapter 2.

To explain these comments more fully, I have attempted in this introduction to trace the trajectory of my thinking about gender as I've participated in or listened to conversations among feminists over the past several decades—particularly, but not exclusively, those feminists working with theories of language often referred to as poststructuralist. I don't claim that what I've written here is a guide to the evolution of feminist thinking; my own engagement with psychoanalysis came very late in the game. As early as the 1970s, some feminists were working with psychoanalytic theory, most of them in philosophy or literature. (There was no shortage of historians' interest in psychoanalysis in the 1960s and 1970s especially, but rarely were they historians of women or feminism.)[11] The great divide among feminists in the 1980s was supposedly between those who took a more sociological approach, working with the concept of gender, and those who opted for psychoanalysis, insisting on sexual difference as a more powerful critical tool. The division was thought to be geopolitical as well as philosophical, separating Anglo-American feminists from their sisters in France and elsewhere in Europe. I never thought of myself as firmly on the gender side, and I knew plenty of Americans who were on the sexual-difference side. Nonetheless, I certainly resisted psychoanalysis for a time, my resistance perhaps reflecting the strength of my disciplinary formation as a historian.

Change came slowly, the product of curiosity, restlessness, and a stubborn desire to hold onto gender as a critical challenge to conventional history. If I had to summarize the change in my thinking as it relates to theorizing gender, I would say that the path is from sex as the known of physical bodies and so the referent for gender, to sexual difference as a permanent quandary—because ultimately unknowable—for modern subjects and so, again, the impossible referent for gender. Gender is, in other words, not the assignment of roles to physically different bodies, but the attribution of meaning to something that always eludes definition. What psychoanalysis helps illuminate is the ultimate unknowability of sexual difference and the nature of the quest for knowledge of it, by way of fantasy, identification, and projection. The vertigo that ensues for the historian deprives her of the certainty of her categories of analysis and leaves her searching only for the right questions to ask.

Sex and Gender

In the beginning it seemed easy. We had Gayle Rubin's brilliant "The Traffic in Women," which took the sex/gender distinction as its premise.[12] Sex was about the division of physical bodies into male and female types; gender was the social or cultural assignment of roles to that established reality. "Gender" meant that the limits placed on women were not physical, but social and historical. From this it followed that existing ascriptions were open to change. Listen to

Natalie Davis in 1974 at one of those early pathbreaking Berkshire Conferences on the History of Women. "Our goal," she said, "is to understand the significance of the *sexes*, of gender groups in the historical past. Our goal is to discover the range in sex roles and in sexual symbolism in different societies and periods, to find out what meanings they had and how they functioned to maintain the social order or to promote change."[13] Change was the crucial point, since as feminists we sought to overturn the limits placed on our aspirations, the unequal treatment we (and other women) experienced. History provided the evidence we needed to make our case. If the roles of women had varied according to class, race, culture, and the time in which they lived, there was nothing inevitable or permanent about our own moment.

The conversation became more complicated with the critique of the sex/gender, nature/culture distinction. Some feminists (among them Judith Butler, Donna Haraway, those associated with the British journal *m/f*) argued that it wasn't enough to point out that physical bodies were not the issue—to put them aside and focus exclusively on culture—because that left in place the idea that sex was a natural and transparent phenomenon and so didn't really contest the legitimating grounds for the assignment of gender roles.[14] The biological reality, in the form of the prior sexual division of bodies kept creeping back into the arguments about culture, disrupting and displacing them. To stop this, sex itself had to be historicized, as the product of social and cultural discourse. The difference of the sexes was the referent that acquired its natural status only retrospectively, as a rationale for the assignment of gender roles. In other words, nature (the difference of the sexes in this instance) was produced by culture as culture's justification—it was not an independent variable, nor an ontological ground, nor the invariant base on which edifices of gender were constructed.

This deconstruction of the sex/gender opposition encouraged important historical work in the history of science and medicine. It also led to investigations of changing regulatory norms and their enforcement; studies of the impact of symbolic structures on the lives and practices of ordinary people; questions about how power and rights related to definitions of masculinity and femininity; and assessments of the ways in which sexual identities were forged within and against social prescriptions. By refusing the notion that sexual identity was determined by biology, it also contributed to the emergence of queer theory. With these developments, gender was no longer seen as a commentary on sex; instead, sex was understood as an effect of gender. Or to put it in other terms, gender and sex were both cultural constructions, creating rather than reflecting a prior reality.

The Limits of Cultural Construction: "Women"

The notion of cultural construction was an important tool of analysis in both the articulation and deconstruction of the sex/gender distinction. Adapted in part from European poststructural linguistic theory and in part from US work in science studies and the social sciences (particularly anthropology), "cultural construction" became a shorthand for the exclusively human origin of the ideas and conceptual categories that organized the realities of experience. In the field of gender studies, it substituted culture for nature in the determination of both sex and gender. Sex, the sexes, gender, and its roles—sexed identities, both collective and individual—were all understood to be the product of culture, by which was most often meant social and political ideologies, whether taken to be expressions of tradition or of modernity. These ideologies were seen to further some powerful interest—status, class, state, sex—as they set forth the norms of culture and society, the justifications for hierarchy, the rules of sexual behavior, and much more. From this perspective, law (whether formal legislation or normative regulation) was not a reflection of nature, as its creators claimed it was, but a producer of the very subjects it regulated. "Legal recognition," Parveen Adams and Jeffrey Minson have noted, "is a real and circular process. It recognizes the things that correspond to the definition it constructs."[15]

This kind of reasoning informed a vast literature on the ways in which men and women, masculinity and femininity, were represented in medicine, science, art (high and low), architecture (domestic and public), literature (children's and adults'), philosophy, law, political theory, public policy, economic theory, and historical texts. The tendency was to assume that subjects (collective or individual) were interpellated by these representations, brought into being by them, whether as unquestioning products of social discourses or protesters against their confining, subordinating, or marginalizing limits.[16]

In much of the historical literature that used the notion of cultural construction, "gender" referred to these representations, to the traits and roles assigned to women (and men), but not to the category of women (or men) itself. I think this had a lot to do with feminist history's ties to the feminist movement and its resulting aim of producing a political subject based on identification with a collectivity of women. There was enormous tension between a theory that stressed the productive work of representation (and so its various articulations) and a political movement that mobilized women on the basis of a universal experience of subordination.

A symptom of this tension was that, even as it gestured to gender as mutable, the historical work done by many feminists assumed a fixed meaning for the categories "women" and "men," or at least didn't problematize them. Instead, it most often took the physical commonality of females as a synonym for a collective entity designated "women." Gender was said to be about the relationship between women and men and assumed to be not only hierarchical, but invariably so: a permanent antagonism that took different forms at different times. And, despite much innovative research on sexuality, gender—at least in historians' writing—most often referred to sexual difference as if it were a known and enduring male/female opposition, a normative (if not distinctly biological) heterosexual coupling, even when homosexuality was the topic being addressed.

It's not that women weren't given a history; of course they were. Ideas about them were said to change, as did their experiences, varying over time and by class, race, ethnicity, culture, religion, and geography. The bountiful literature of women's social history is full of important distinctions that insist on the specificity of the experiences of working or peasant or lesbian or medieval or Jewish or African American or Muslim or Latina or Eastern European women. But however much they attend to the quotidian lives of diverse populations, these differences take for granted what Denise Riley calls an "underlying continuity of real women above whose constant bodies changing aerial descriptions dance."[17] (Gender was taken to be those dancing "aerial descriptions.") Paradoxically, the history of women kept "women" outside history. And the result is that "women" as a natural phenomenon (one side of that permanent sexual division) was reinscribed, even as we asserted that they were discursively constructed. To put it another way, the sex/gender binary, which defined gender as the social assignment of meaning to biologically given sex differences, remained in place despite a generation of scholarship aimed at deconstructing the opposition. As long as "women" continue to "form a passive backdrop to changing conceptions of gender," our history rests on a biological foundation that feminists, at least in theory, want to contest.[18]

There were, of course, some historians (influenced importantly by Michel Foucault) who did interrogate the different possible meanings of the terms "men" and "women." Riley's work is at once exemplary and a rare instance of the historicizing of the category of women. Her *Am I that Name? Feminism and the Category of "Women" in History* is addressed to feminists and focuses on the difficulty posed for us by the need to simultaneously insist on and refuse the identity of "women." This, she maintains, is not a liability, but the condition that gives rise to feminism. " 'Women' is indeed an unstable category . . . this instability has a historical foundation, and . . . feminism is the site of the systematic fighting-out of that instability."[19] It is not only that there are different kinds of women assembled under the term, but also that the collective identity means different things at different times. Even individual women are not always conscious of being a woman. The identity, Riley says, does not pervade us and so is "inconstant, and can't provide an ontological foundation."[20] "The body" doesn't provide that foundation either, since it is a concept that must be "read in relation to whatever else supports and surrounds it."[21] "For all its corporeality," Riley points out, the body is not "an originating point nor yet a terminus; it is a result or an effect."[22]

The absence of an ontological foundation might suggest that it is futile to try to study women's history: if there are no women, some of Riley's critics have complained, how can there be women's history or, for that matter, feminism?[23] In fact, by making "women" the object of historical investigation, Riley engages in that vertigo-inducing critical examination Certeau called for, albeit not in explicitly psychoanalytic terms. Her more Foucauldian genealogy asks when the category "women" comes under discussion and in what terms, and she points to the ways in which, at different historical moments, there have been different kinds of openings created for feminist claims: "The arrangements of people under the banners of 'men' or 'women' are enmeshed in the histories of other concepts too, including those of 'the social' and 'the body.' And that has profound repercussions for feminism."[24] Riley shows how, in early modern Europe, notions of the androgynous soul defined one kind of relation of "women" to humanity, whereas by the eighteenth century, attention to nature and the body led to an increasing emphasis on women's sexuality. As "the social" found a place between "the domestic" and "the political" in the nineteenth century, it "established 'women' as a new kind of sociological collectivity."[25] And, of course, until individuals were defined as political subjects, there could be no claim for citizenship for women. It's not just that women have different kinds of possibilities in their lives, but that "women" is something different in each of these moments. There is no essence of womanhood (or of manhood) to provide a stable subject for our histories; there are only successive iterations of a word that doesn't have a fixed referent and so doesn't always mean the same thing. If this is true of "women," it is also true of "gender." The relationship posited between male and female, masculine and feminine, is not predictable; we cannot assume that we know in advance what it is. This is so both at the level of social understanding and, in a different—but connected—way, at the level of a subject's self-identification.

The Limits of Cultural Construction: Causality

Even if, as Riley so cogently argued, "women" is an unstable category, this doesn't mean that it has no historical existence. It may be transitory, coming into and out of view, but it exists in its temporal context, with important effects. It serves to organize women in its image, either as willing or protesting subjects. Either way, we think of women as culturally constructed—that is, as fitting more or less comfortably into a socially specified way of being.

The notion of cultural or social construction was criticized from the start (whenever that was) by theorists who recognized its philosophical limits. Judith Butler describes the "problematic of construction" this way: "What is constructed is of necessity prior to construction, even as there appears no access to this prior moment except through construction."[26]

Some psychoanalytic critics went further, objecting not only to the constructivist model of causality, but also to its failure to take psychic processes into account. Here is Joan Copjec, a Lacanian, in 1989:

> The social system of representation is conceived as lawful, regulatory, and on this account the *cause* of the subject. . . . The subject is assumed to be already virtually there in the social and to come into being by actually wanting what the social laws want it to want. The construction of the subject depends, then, on the subject's taking social representations as images of its own ideal being.[27]

Copjec argues that such a view missed "the essential fact of language's duplicity, that is, the fact that whatever it says can be denied. This duplicity insures that the subject will *not* come into being as language's determinate meaning."[28] Instead, Copjec maintains, it was "the very impossibility of representing the subject to the subject . . . that founds the subject's identity":

> We are constructed, then, not in conformity to social laws, but in response to our inability to conform to or see ourselves as defined by social limits. Though we are defined and limited *historically*, the absence of the real, which founds these limits, is not *historicizable*. It is only this distinction, which informs the Lacanian definition of cause, that allows us to think the construction of the subject without being thereby obliged to reduce her *to* the images social discourses construct *of* her.[29]

The subject is not the determined product of the law, but "rather something that escapes the law and its determination, something we can't manage to put our finger on. . . . This indeterminate something . . . that causes the subject has historical specificity (it is the product of a specific discursive order), but no historical content. The subject is the product of history without being the fulfillment of a historical demand."[30] Or, as Certeau puts it, "the labor by which the subject *authorizes* his own existence is of a kind other than the labor for which he receives *permission* to exist. The Freudian process attempts to articulate this difference."[31]

Certeau may be referring to Freud's short essay, "Constructions in Analysis," but whether he is or not, it is useful to consider it here. For Freud "construction" means not cultural causality or interpellation, but the analyst's not always accurate or successful attempt to "make out what has been forgotten from the traces" of memory unearthed in the analytic process.[32] Constructions are more than interpretations, he notes, because they are attempts to systematically put together pieces of a patient's forgotten earlier history (akin to an archaeological recon- struction of a pot from shards found in a dig). Any construction is necessarily incomplete "since it covers only a small fragment of the forgotten events."[33] And it is subject to distortion and delusion on both sides of the analytic process.[34] In this sense, construction is hardly a fully accurate account but instead is a continuing effort, necessarily incomplete, a way of elucidating the complexities that notions of cultural construction typically neglect or ignore. Freud's use of the term nicely inverts that meaning of "construction," defining it instead as a way of getting at the repressions, displacements, and fantasies that color a patient's self-representations (and that are often taken literally by those invoking cultural constructions of the subject). Jean Laplanche and Jean-Bertrand Pontalis comment that "in the last reckoning, the term 'construction' raises the whole problem of uncon- scious structure and of the structuring role of the treatment."[35]

The question of the unconscious and fantasy returns us to Cop- jec's crucial point. I would say that the subject's being is woven in fantasies that attempt to provide substance for that "indeterminate something," that absence or kernel of "non-sense" (because it is an absence, it can have no historical content) that follows from the impossibility of representing the subject to herself. Identity, such as it is, is not the "imitation of any ideal vision," but a response to "the very impossibility of ever making visible this missing part."[36] It's not the case that a fully formed self is resisting the impositions of the social order or measuring what it knows of its true self against a misimpres- sion on the outside, as some liberal theories of autonomous individ- ual will would have it. Rather, what we have is the idea of a psyche that has no access to certain confirmation of its identity—it doesn't "really" exist. Instead, it depends on some others or Other for completion or recognition. But these others, whether objects or people, are not free of the subject's projective fantasies or their own. Moreover, these fantasies express drives and desires not under the control of conscious reasoning.

Coming at the question from a slightly different angle, but with remarkable resonance to the thinking of these theorists, Foucault also refuses a simple notion of cultural determination. The modern subject is "always open, never finally delimited, yet constantly traversed."[37] He continues:

> When he tries to define himself as a living being, he can uncover his own beginning only against the background of a life which itself began long before him; when he attempts to re-apprehend himself as a labouring being, he cannot bring even the most rudimentary forms of such a being to light except within a human time and space which have been previously institutionalized, and previously subjugated by society; and when he attempts to define his essence as a speaking subject, prior to any effectively constituted language, all he ever finds is the previously unfolded possibility of language.[38]

The process is more dynamic, complex, and unpredictable than simple notions of cultural construction would have it:

> The signifying chain by which the unique experience of the individual is constituted is perpendicular to the formal system on the basis of which the significations of a culture are constituted: at any given instant, the structure proper to individual experience finds a certain number of possible choices (and of excluded possibilities) in the systems of the society; inversely, at each of their points of choice the social structures encounter a certain number of possible individuals (and others who are not [possible])—just as the linear structure of language always produces a possible choice between several words or several phonemes at any given moment (but excludes others).[39]

Foucault offers this description toward the end of *The Order of Things* as part of a discussion of the relationship between ethnology and psychoanalysis—the two "branches of knowledge investigating man" that operate on a "perpetual principle of dissatisfaction" with established forms of knowledge.[40] Both fields, he suggests, stand in critical relationship to the empirical human sciences, exposing the unconscious dimensions that escape them. They are "counter-sciences," "which does not mean that they are less 'rational' or 'objective' than the others, but that they flow in the opposite direction, that they lead them back to their epistemological basis, and that they ceaselessly 'unmake' that very man who is creating and re-creating his positivity in the human sciences."[41]

The psychic dimension of human existence cannot be reduced simply to exposures to implicit meaning or to interpretations of resistance and defense. The great virtue of the Freudian approach, for Foucault, is that it illuminates the "three figures by means of which life, with its functions and norms, attains its foundation in the mute repetition of Death, conflicts and rules [attain] their foundation in the naked opening of Desire, significations and systems [attain] their foundation in a language which is at the same time Law."[42] He continues: "It is indeed true that this Death, and this Desire, and this Law can never meet within the knowledge that traverses in its positivity the empirical domain of man; but the reason for this is that they designate the conditions of possibility of all knowledge about man."[43] That knowledge has to do not with empirical information, but rather with that which cannot be known: "what is there and yet is hidden . . . what exists with the mute solidity of a thing, of a text closed in upon itself, or of a blank space in a visible text."[44] "Psychoanalysis moves toward the moment—by definition inaccessible to any theoretical knowledge of man, to any continuous apprehension in terms of signification, conflict or function—at which the contents of consciousness articulate themselves, or rather stand gaping, upon man's finitude."[45] Elizabeth Weed suggests that "the scene of man's finitude finds powerful staging in the psychoanalytic theory of sexual difference."[46]

Sexual Difference

For psychoanalysis, the conundrum of identity revolves around the question of sexual difference. The term "sexual difference" is not technically part of psychoanalytic vocabulary but comes from feminists, particularly those working with the theories of Jacques Lacan.[47]

It refers to the complex process by which sexed identities are formulated, to the difficulty—if not the impossibility—of finally answering the questions that sex and sexuality pose: Where do I come from? What do these bodies mean? How are the differences between them to be explained? What is to be done with sexual desire? Butler offers this definition: "Sexual difference is the site where a question concerning the relation of the biological to the cultural is posed and reposed, where it must and can be posed, but where it cannot, strictly speaking, be answered. Understood as a border concept, sexual difference has psychic, somatic, and social dimensions that are never quite collapsible into one another but are not for that reason ultimately distinct."[48]

For Freud, sexual difference is brought into being with the Oedipus complex and the threat of castration. This is the point at which a child realizes that one cannot be both male and female; the child is given stories about this (the myths of his or her culture, with its normative rules and regulations) and ponders what it all means. The unconscious fantasies play with, adapt, transgress, and exceed cultural norms; they find expression in drives and desires that cannot be entirely correlated either with conscious intention or the body's materiality. Infantile and childhood fantasies persist into adulthood, evident in dreams and brought to life by some tangible experience or inadvertent stimulus. They become incorporated, albeit invisibly, into the conscious ways in which we perceive the world and give accounts of ourselves.

The fact that one cannot be both male and female is puzzling and, indeed, troubling, but it does not restrict identification or limit the operations of desire. As Butler puts it, "a woman may find the phantasmatic remainder of her father in another woman or substitute her desire for her mother in a man, at which point a certain crossing of heterosexual and homosexual desires operate at once."[49] These identifications, imagined resemblances, work with and against what Lacan referred to as the symbolic, a structure of signifiers that establishes the order into which human subjects are inserted. Although some followers of Lacan take the symbolic to be an immutable structure that legislates a singular dimorphic meaning for sexual difference, I take the interpretation by Laplanche and Pontalis to be more apt. On the one hand, they suggest, the symbolic is "the law upon which this order is based"; on the other hand, since signifiers cannot be "permanently bound to the signified," the boundaries are permeable and do not irrevocably determine who the subject will be.[50] Thus, there is no necessary correspondence between the anatomy of men and women and the psychic positions of masculinity and femininity that they arrive at. Sexual difference, Weed writes, "is a term that could signify *at the same time* the coercive psychic positioning in the symbolic and the impossibility of ever taking one's sexual place."[51] It is in the interaction between the symbolic (signifiers of the law) and the imaginary (narcissistic identifications with others) around the unsolvable riddle of sexual difference (in Lacanian terms, the real; Copjec's kernel of nonsense) that psychoanalysis interrogates; the process is dynamic for both subjects and analysts. Its effects make history.

An example may be helpful here to get beyond the abstraction of some of these terms. It comes from work I have done on nineteenth- and twentieth-century French feminists who challenged the association of masculinity and universalism in republican theories of citizenship.[52] Sometimes appealing to promises of equality for all, these feminists insisted that their humanity made them eligible for citizenship; sexed bodies were beside the point. At other times, they argued that the universal individual was not singular, but included both males and females; the recognition that bodies were sexed would make them, again, beside the point. For all the ingenuity of their arguments, for all their logical plausibility, these feminists nonetheless found it next to impossible to refute the deeply held belief that differences of sex precluded genuine equality. This does not mean that they failed to change laws or raise awareness of discrimination against women; it does mean that the founding premises of sexual difference persisted in other forms. Getting the vote, for instance, did not improve women's access to political office or to leadership positions in industry. The law that was supposed to guarantee that access was based on a notion not of gender equality, but of the complementarity of the sexes—with the heterosexual couple as the model.

Weed suggests that we look to the symbolic, an unconscious dimension, to account for the persistence of these ideas. She follows Lacan's adaptation of Freud's notion of the Oedipus complex, which says that masculinity and femininity are defined in asymmetrical relationships to the phallus—the signifier of desire in modern Western cultures. According to Lacan, both masculine and feminine are assumed to be castrated, but in different ways. The feminine is already castrated since she lacks the penis, which is mistakenly equated with the phallus. The masculine is both castrated by the paternal prohibition against sexual relations with the mother, but also convinced that someone with whom he identifies (the primal father, his own father, or the imagined lawgiver in whom phallus and penis are taken to be the same) is exempt from castration. This makes the masculine position a paradoxical one. The masculine subject is simultaneously castrated and exempt from the symbolic law; he is simultaneously singular and universal. The feminine subject is also castrated but has no access to this phallic exception. Weed puts it this way: "In psychical life, *la femme*, in her infinite lack, cannot be generalized; only *l'homme* can be taken for the universal."[53] She then links this to the ways in which, since the Enlightenment, the abstract individual of political theory has been presumed to be masculine, while the feminine has been synonymous with the particular and the concrete. (Simone de Beauvoir expressed this contrast in terms of man's transcendence, his disembodiment, and woman's immanence, her confinement to her body.)[54] The language of this political theory, and the changing and diverse practices justified in its name, are the effects of the symbolic structure of sexual difference.

This is not to say that real men and women are fully determined by these concepts. (Precisely because the phallus is not the penis, there is no necessary correspondence between anatomy and psychic positioning.) If they were, there would be no feminist movements, no challenges to the prevailing order of things. It is to say, however, that the concepts provide the language through which identities are formed, the unconscious foundations on which social practices are implemented, but also—since language is mobile and, in Copjec's terms, duplicitous—challenged and changed. The operations of fantasy come into play here as fantasy enables challenge and change. Fantasy offers historians a way of thinking the history of sexuality beyond the narrow confines of identity politics, comparative social movements, and national or transnational sexual cultures.[55]

Fantasy

In some uses of the idea of cultural construction, gender is seen as a simple effect of power; some rational goal is at stake in the assignment of traits and functions to women and men: economic exploitation, political dominance, imperial conquest, interests of state, race, class, status, or sex. By referring them to gender (literally or metaphorically), the hierarchies and inequalities are naturalized, made to seem part of the order of nature. But how do these appeals achieve their effect? What is it that they are appealing to? Fantasy may offer an answer here because people are not simply rational, goal-oriented beings, but subjects of unconscious desire—desire articulated in terms of, but not defined by, the symbolic, in which the relationship between signifier and signified can never be clear. Thus people aren't mobilized according to purely objective interests, but rather according to interests created for them by collective fantasies. Such fantasies infuse interest with desire and seem to provide an answer to the impossible question of identity, to the subjects' quest for wholeness and coherence, by merging them into a group. Group membership provides the illusion of wholeness; it appears to give sense to that elusive kernel of non-sense. Mutual recognition allays the psychic anxieties of identity.[56]

From this perspective, feminist movements are not the inevitable expression of the socially constructed category of women, but the means for achieving that identity. The fantasy being appealed to is a promise of wholeness and completeness, adequate representation; the terms of appeal and the political, social, and economic interests identified as objects of need or desire are matters for historical investigation. None of this is to deny the social fact of feminist movements (or any other political identity movement), nor to question the existence of active political subjects (feminists or citizens, for example). It is to suggest that psychoanalysis points us usefully to the unconscious dimensions of these phenomena, to the fact that they owe at least some of their existence to the operations of fantasies that can never fully satisfy the desire, or secure the representation, they seek to provide.

The unconscious workings of individual psyches may begin as what Laplanche calls "enigmatic signifiers," nonverbal messages communicated to infants whose meaning is never clear.[57] But they are not forged entirely independently of what later becomes conscious awareness of normative categories and their enforcement. Normative categories are not direct reflections of the symbolic, nor are they simply rational statements of desirable identification. Rather, they are products of historically specific discursive orders, contextually varying attempts to enact the symbolic, to eliminate the psychic confusion or anxiety that sexual difference generates and that is often addressed by fantasy. Fantasy weaves together infantile, childhood, and adult desire in a labile mix, expressed variously in dreams, reveries, and stories. It is made coherent in what Freud refers to as "secondary revision," which François Duparc defines as the "rearrangement of the seemingly incoherent elements of the dream into a form serviceable for narration. This involves logical and temporal reorganization in obedience to the principles of noncontradiction, temporal sequence, and causality which characterize the secondary processes of conscious thought."[58] It is, of course, as Ben Kafka points out, precisely these narrations that historians begin with. Reading back from them with attention to their specificity and idiosyncrasy is the challenge we face, and for which we need the tools of psychoanalytic theory.[59]

Normative categories seek to bring subjects' fantasies in line with cultural myth and social organization, but they never entirely succeed. These categories are themselves not free of phantasmatic investments. When, to take one glaring instance, feminists campaigned for the Equal Rights Amendment to the US Constitution in the late 1970s and early 1980s, the opposition regularly offered the specter of mandatory single-sex public toilets as a warning of the worst dangers of the amendment. In some lurid scenarios, bathrooms became the site of rape (violations of privacy, intrusions into women's private places, were projected), racial invasion (black men entering white women's "rooms"), and miscegenation. Only by maintaining the boundaries of sexual and racial difference could the catastrophic fulfillment of transgressive desire be avoided.[60]

Gender, then, is the study of the relationship between the normative and the psychic. Gender consists of the historically specific and finally uncontrollable articulations that aim to settle the confusions associated with sexual difference by directing fantasy to some political or social end: group mobilization, nation building, support for a specific family structure, ethnic consolidation, or religious practice.[61] To give one example, the analysis of male dominance in its different forms profits from such a psychoanalytic approach, one that asks how links between social and psychic anxiety are being forged in the denigration or exaltation of women's sexuality in relation to men's, in the boundaries that maintain differences of sex, and in phantasmatic warnings about the consequences of altering or breaching those boundaries.

The Fantasy of Feminist History

Psychoanalytic theory does not provide a causality to substitute for cultural construction, at least not in the way I want to use it. Instead, it reformulates many of my original questions about gender and opens up new ways of thinking about them. This new approach takes gender to be the history of the articulations of the masculine/feminine, male/female distinction, whether in terms of bodies, roles, or psychological traits. It does not assume the prior existence of the masculine/feminine, male/female distinction, but rather examines the complicated, contradictory, and ambivalent way it has emerged in different social and political discourses. Neither does it assume that normative discourses determine the way subjects identify themselves. Fantasy disrupts these kinds of correlations, refusing the certainty of disciplined history's categories. In their place, there is the elusive pursuit of language, not only as the conscious expression of ideas, but as the revelation of unconscious processes. We have to ask how, under what conditions, and with what fantasies the identities of men and women—which so many historians take to be self-evident—are articulated and recognized. The categories then will no longer precede the analysis but emerge in the course of it. Certeau puts it this way: "History can be construed as the gesture of a new beginning. At least this is what is shown by the form of history that is already constituted by Freudian praxis. Finally, it locates its veritable meaning not in the elucidations with which it replaces former representations, but in the ever-unfinished *act* of elucidation."[62]

It is finally the emphasis on the unknowable and its endless pursuit that I take from psychoanalysis. One of the most appealing aspects of this kind of thinking is that it unsettles certainty, calls into question our ability ever finally to know. In the words of William Langer, a historian of an earlier generation (who scandalized his colleagues when, in his presidential address to the American Historical Association in 1957, he called for a turn to psychoanalysis), "we must be ready, from time to time, to take flyers into the unknown."[63] Neither our categories of analysis nor the evidence we accumulate can furnish an ultimate meaning for sexual difference, which explains, among other things, the anxiety with which established boundaries are policed and the disciplinary power brought to bear on those seen to transgress established limits. We can ask how sexual difference is signified, what those significations reveal in their ambivalences and instabilities, and what effects they have had. We can try to lay bare the fantasies woven in support of these significations and speculate about the unconscious wishes they express; we can marvel at the human capacity to create variations on the themes of sex, sexual difference, and sexuality; and we can interrogate our own investments in these stories. There is, of course, a political aspect to this kind of inquiry, though it is not utopian in any final sense. The elusiveness of sexual difference is both unrealizable and, for that very reason, historical. It is a quest that never ends. As such, it interrupts the certainty of established categories, thus creating openings to the future. Our histories become something like Freud's description of "a day-dream or phantasy," in which "past, present and future are strung together, as it were, on the thread of the wish that runs through them."[64]

My fantasy of feminist history, the one that animates this book, is of a quest for understanding that is never fully satisfied with its own results. It is one in which critical reading replaces the operations of classification, in which the relationship between past and present is not taken for granted but considered a problem to be explored, and in which the thinking of the historian is an object of inquiry along with that of her subjects. This implies that Professor Parker's "madness" and "passion" are to be found on both sides of the analytic process. And for that reason, as Certeau points out, "analytic practice is always an act of risk. It never eliminates surprise. It cannot be identified with the accomplishment of a norm. The ambiguity of a set of words could never be brought forward solely by the 'application' of a law. Knowledge never guarantees this 'benefit.'"[65]

1. Feminism's History

IN 1974, LOIS BANNER AND MARY HARTMAN published a book of essays they called *Clio's Consciousness Raised*.[1] Consisting of papers from the 1973 Berkshire Conference on Women's History, it was a rallying cry for many of us, an assertion of our intention to make women proper objects of historical study. If the muse of history had too long sung the praises of men ("glorifying the countless mighty deeds of ancient times for the instruction of posterity"), it was now time to bestow a similar glory on women.[2] The second of the nine daughters of Zeus and Mnemosyne (the goddess of memory), Clio's special province was history (or epic poetry, a historical genre in ancient Greece). Our challenge to her seemed simple: make women's stories central to the memory she transmitted to mortals. In order to ease her task, we would supply the materials she needed, the histories of the lives and activities of women.

Of course, no challenge to the gods is simple, nor was our effort without hubris, for we were presuming to tell Clio what to say. The muses have meted out dire punishment to those who sought to interfere or compete with them. The Pierides were turned into magpies, ducks, and other squawking birds for trying to outsing the muses.

When the sirens claimed to sing better, the muses plucked their feathers to make crowns for themselves. The minstrel Thamyris was blinded and sent to Hades for having boasted that he could sing more beautifully. And, less cruelly, the muses had the last word when Prometheus claimed that he, not they, had created the letters of the alphabet. This could have been a matter of dispute, the chroniclers tell us, "had not the Muses invented all tales, including that of Prometheus."[3]

Our goal was not so much to compete with Clio as to become her agents, though there is always an element of competition in such identification. Like her, we wanted to tell edifying stories whose import went beyond their literal content to reveal some larger truth about human relationships—in our case, about gender and power. Like her, we wanted to be recognized as the source of those stories. Like her, too, we wanted all of history as our province; we were not just adding women to an existing body of stories, we wanted to change the way the stories would be told. Clio was our inspiration, but we wanted also to be her, inspiring others to document the memory we were uncovering.

The last few decades have seen some progress toward these goals. Of course they haven't been completely achieved: neither women's history nor women historians have become fully equal players in the discipline, and we have by no means rewritten all the stories. Indeed, the temporal and geographic unevenness of our accomplishment—far greater success in modern European and American history than in ancient, medieval, early modern, or non-Western history; far more success in introducing women into the picture than in reconceiving of it in terms of gender—clearly shows that there is more to be done. Still, the gains are undeniable. Unlike Clio, we can't punish those who would deny our accomplishment; nor can we afford to be amused by the folly of those brothers of Prometheus who claim to be the real innovators, treating us as imitators or usurpers. (We still get angry.) We can, however, point to an enormous written corpus, an imposing institutional presence, a substantial list of journals, and a foothold in popular consciousness that was unimaginable when Banner and Hartman published their book. If we have not taken over history, we have claimed a rightful position in it; once viewed as pretenders, we now have legitimate claim to Clio's inspiration.

But legitimacy, for those who began as revolutionaries, is always an ambiguous accomplishment. It is at once a victory and a sellout, the triumph of critique and its abandonment. This is difficult for feminists who, despite all the derision cast on them by socialists in the nineteenth and twentieth centuries, have been revolutionaries dedicated to overturning patriarchy, breaking the oppressive chains of sexism, liberating women from the stereotypes that confine them, and bringing them onto the stage of history. The realization of at least some positive change since the early 1970s—which I have just characterized for historians of women as gaining a legitimate claim to Clio's inspiration—has produced some ambivalence and uncertainty about the future. Have we won or lost? Have we been changed by our success? What does the move from embattled outsider to recognized insider portend for our collective identity? Has our presence transformed the discipline, or have we simply been absorbed into it? Ought we to be content with maintaining and reproducing what we have gained, or should we be responding to new challenges that may threaten our legitimate standing? Does women's history have a future, or is it history? How might we imagine its future? These are questions also being asked about women's studies and feminism.

As the millennium approached, a number of forums were organized in the United States to speculate about the future. To cite only two examples: In 1997 I edited a special issue of the journal *differences* called "Women's Studies on the Edge"—a title meant to evoke Pedro Almodovar's film *Women on the Verge of a Nervous Breakdown.* Although we chose it playfully, the allusion turned out to be an apt characterization of how edgy some of us feel when asked to think about the future.[4] In 1999 the *Journal of Women's History* organized a terrific intergenerational exchange among the Americanists Anne Firor Scott, Sara Evans, Elizabeth Faue, and Susan Cahn.[5] (The four constitute a lineage: Scott was Evans's teacher; Evans taught Faue and Cahn.) In an otherwise rich and wide-ranging discussion, these historians kept avoiding the topic of the future, although that was the stated purpose of the conversation. At one point, Scott confessed that in thinking about "where women's history should, or might, go from here," she found herself "running up against a wall" ("Part 1," 29). Faue thought that we needed to "take time out to dream," to exercise imagination and creativity to get beyond the impasse ("Part 2," 211). But Evans summed up what appeared to be a general reluctance among them. "Ah, the future," she sighed. "I agree . . . that this is the part of the conversation I find most perilous" (205).

Futures

Why would the future of a successful movement be so difficult to envision?

In some ways we already know the answer—it's a form of social movement analysis. An aging generation of feminist scholar-activists looks back nostalgically on its wild youth, wondering (but not daring to ask aloud) if all the gains we've made were worth it. The institutionalization of women's history implies its end as a campaign. Our research and professional activities seem to have lost their purposive political edge and their sense of dedication to building something larger than an individual career. The community of feminist scholars, whose vitality was manifest in fierce divisions no less than in shared commitments, now seems diffuse. And, at least among historians of women, the theoretical and political stakes no longer seem as high, while disagreements seem more personal or generational. If there is relief at the end of the need to conspire in late-night strategy sessions and to constantly have to justify one's scholarship and that of one's students to skeptical or hostile colleagues—as well as pleasure in the quantity, quality, and diversity of work produced under the rubric of women's history—there is also a sense of loss. For many of us, being embattled was energizing; it elicited strategic and intellectual creativity unmatched by our earlier experiences in graduate school. Inspired by Clio, we sought to change the received version of history. Appeals to Clio consolidated our identity as historians and feminists; activism confirmed agency. We were producers of new knowledge and transmitters of revised memory, fashioning tales to inspire ourselves and the generations to come—all in the face of opponents more formidable than the Pierides or the sirens, opponents who had the power to discipline us for what they took to be our pretensions and misdeeds. No longer insurgents, we have become disciplinarians, and I suspect that inevitably there's something of a letdown in this change of identity. It is one thing to criticize disciplinary power from the outside, another to be inside, committed to the teaching of established bodies of scholarship. That kind of teaching necessarily seeks to reproduce feminist history in rising generations of students, but it is often resistant to the kind of critical challenges that was its defining characteristic.

As academic feminism has gained institutional credibility, it also has seemed to lose its close connection to the political movement that inspired it. In the 1970s and 1980s, we were the knowledge-producing arm of a broad-based feminist movement devoted to radical social change. During the 1990s, there were critical attacks on, and guilt-ridden condemnations of, the diminished contact between scholars and the grass roots, as well as injunctions to maintain or rebuild those ties. But that effort has foundered. This is not, as is sometimes alleged, because feminist scholars have retreated to ivory towers; the opposition between academic and political feminism was always a mischaracterization. Rather, it is because the political movement itself has become fragmented, has dispersed into specific areas of activism. This does not mean, as some journalists have claimed, that feminism is dead. In fact, concerns about the status and condition of different kinds of women have infiltrated many more realms of law and policy than was the case at the height of the movement, just as questions about gender have bled into areas of study that were resistant to feminism in the early days of women's studies.[6]

Discontinuous, individually coordinated strategic operations with other groups have replaced a continuous struggle on behalf of women represented as a singular entity. This change is tied to the loss of a grand teleological narrative of emancipation, one that allowed us to conceive of the cumulative effect of our efforts: freedom and equality were the inevitable outcomes of human struggle, we believed, and that belief gave coherence to our actions, defined us as participants in a progressive movement. We were on the side of redemptive history. Although discontinuity and dispersed strategic operations are eminently political in nature (and, for a younger generation, a familiar way of operating), the loss of the continuity that came with the notion of history as inevitably progressive helps explain the difficulty an older generation has in imagining a future. They take discontinuity to be regressive—the opposite of progressive, which indeed it was for those who watched fascism in Europe destroy liberal institutions in the 1930s—when in the twenty-first century, discontinuity seems to me to be more closely allied to radical (Left) critiques.

Another aspect of the successful institutionalization of women's history is the dulling of the critical edge that comes with being on the margin. There was much debate in the 1980s, perhaps a bit more among literary scholars than historians, about the ultimate benefits of integration. Was the absence of women in the curriculum simply a gap in knowledge that needed to be filled? Or did it reveal something more pernicious about the patriarchal or phallogocentric organization of knowledge itself? What kind of impact would women's studies have on the university? Would we simply provide information now lacking, or would we change the very nature of what counted as knowledge? And were these necessarily contradictory aims? "As long as women's studies doesn't question the existing model of the university," Jacques Derrida told a meeting of the Pembroke Center seminar in 1984, "it risks to be just another cell in the university beehive."[7] Some feminists insisted that, by definition, a female presence in history textbooks and history departments, from which women had usually been excluded, was a subversion of the status quo. Wasn't becoming visible itself a challenge to the prevailing historical orthodoxy that maintained women's absence from politics and history? Others of us argued that the radical potential of women's history would be lost without a thoroughgoing critique of the presumptions of the discipline: for example, its notion that agency is somehow inherent in the wills of individuals; its inattention to language in the construction of subjects and their identities; and its lack of reflection on the implicit interpretive powers of narrative. It is significant, I think, that the lively reform-versus-revolution debate has receded from discussions among women's historians. With at least some measure of reform achieved, the troubling issues now are more mundane: overspecialization, overproduction, and fragmentation, all of which undermine the cohesiveness of the community of feminist scholars and make impossible any mastery of the entire corpus of women's history. Even those who do share a common reading list are more likely to debate the merits of a particular interpretation than to ask how it advances a feminist critical agenda. Preoccupied with the details of administering programs, implementing or adjusting curricular offerings, supervising undergraduate majors, and placing doctoral candidates, we imagine the future as a continuation of the present rather than as a liberation from it.

Still another reason it is so difficult to look forward is that the university into which we have been incorporated is itself undergoing major structural change. Having been critics on the outside, we are now advocates on the inside, looking to preserve the institution—as a faculty-governed, tenure-granting, knowledge-producing space of critical inquiry—from those who would reorganize it according to corporate models in which, as Bill Readings puts it, "clients are sold services for a fee."[8] The need to prevent the "ruin" of the university casts feminists more often as defenders of the status quo than as agents of change. The temptation is to use our analyses of power to shore up what we've won, protecting it from erosion by chief executive officers in the guise of presidents and by trustees who treat ideas as commodities and scholars as their retailers, rather than producers. There is a new need to cooperate with colleagues, some of whom were once our adversaries, on a common agenda committed to the preservation of the academy as we have known it. In this context, demands for radical reform of the entire enterprise seem out of place, if not dangerous. Instead, we vigilantly guard the boundaries of our field, protesting unfair distributions of resources, alert to incursions on our turf from new and sexier areas of scholarship, and wary of surveyors who might redraw the maps we have followed so well. Our protectionism sometimes even leads us to collaborate with those administrators who are intent on commodifying the life of the mind. If we are indeed one of the cells in the university beehive, our interest now is in maintaining both the position of that cell and the health of the entire hive. Defense of the status quo, and of the humanist principles that underlie it, seems far more urgent than holding onto dreams of radical transformation. We are, I think, witnessing a version of what Nancy Cott, referring to the postsuffrage era, called "the grounding of modern feminism"—the practical implementation, which necessarily falls short, of ideals and emancipatory claims; the acceptance of what is, instead of a continued quest for what ought to be; the domestication of fervent desire.[9]

Fervent Desire

Fervent desire is a gift of the muses, a kind of madness that takes over, igniting and transforming the subject. According to Plato, "it seizes a tender, virgin soul and stimulates it to rapt passionate expression . . . but if any man come to the gates of poetry without the madness of the Muses, persuaded that skill alone will make him a good poet [we might substitute "a good historian by discipline"], then shall he and his works of sanity . . . be brought to naught."[10]

Our careful analyses of the structural causes and effects of the rise and fall of social movements do not leave much room for divine madness, nor do they let us see its operations. But if we are working with or as Clio, we need to take it into account. And when we do look for it, we find evidence that it matters in our ability to imagine the future. Over and over again, in the cross-generational conversation published in the *Journal of Women's History*, the four historians describe their attraction to women's history in terms of passion, signifying the inspiration and arousal elicited by the muses.[11] Evans talks of women's history as "a life-absorbing passion" (11); Faue recounts the awakening in graduate school of her "passion" for women's history (13) and the terrific excitement of sharing "new words, new ideas, and new experiences jumbled together" in "wild cacophony" (23); Scott recalls an "impassioned statement" she made at a meeting of the Organization of American Historians, calling for attention to those whom traditional historical accounts had overlooked (19); and Cahn refers to her "passionate" pursuit of feminism and history (15). Looking at the current reduction in tenure-track faculty positions, Evans worries that students with "a great passion for women's history" will be deterred by the job market from following their desire (214).

It is, of course, possible that passion here has a rote, even moralizing, quality. But I think it actually connotes deep feeling with an erotic component. The world being evoked by the notion of passion is the "female world of love and ritual" that Carroll Smith-Rosenberg so brilliantly described in 1975. Existing within the terms of normative heterosexuality (indeed, defined by them), it was nonetheless deeply "homosocial," and thrilling for that reason.[12] Bonnie Anderson and Leila Rupp have portrayed international feminist movements in similar terms.[13] Women's history, before its institutionalization, was like those worlds of the nineteenth and early twentieth centuries. All that libidinal energy devoted to women as objects of inquiry, subjects of rights, students, colleagues, and friends—which was enhanced by the excitement of trespass. We were boldly claiming a previously denied right of access to the field of history. Men were present, to be sure, as targets of anger, as wielders of power whose resistance or indifference needed to be overcome, even as allies; but they were largely irrelevant to the experience of the movement. Men were the Other against whom our political and affective community was defined.

Some of the difficulty we now have in thinking about the future seems to me to be a symptom of melancholy, an unwillingness to let go of the highly charged affect of the homosocial world we have lost— indeed an unwillingness even to acknowledge that it has been lost. The melancholic wants to reverse time, to continue living as before. Melancholia, Freud tells us, is a "reaction to the loss of a loved person, or to the loss of some abstraction which has taken the place of one, such as one's country, liberty, an ideal, and so on."[14] Unlike mourning, which consciously addresses the loss, melancholy is an unconscious process; the lost object is not understood as such. Instead, the melancholic identifies with the lost object and displaces her grief and anger onto herself. In the melancholic, "the shadow of the object fell upon the ego, and the latter could henceforth be judged . . . as though it were . . . the forsaken object."[15] The judgment is harsh, and the normal process by which libido, or sexual energy, is directed to another object is interrupted. Turned in on herself, the melancholic dwells only in the past. To be able to think about the future means to be willing to separate oneself from the lost object, avow the loss, and find a new object for passionate attachment.[16]

There is no question that when women's history came of age, the intensity of the passion associated with the campaign to secure its legitimacy waned. However much remains to be done in this unevenly developed field, the early thrills of discovery no longer drive our work in the same way. For one thing, although women's studies programs remain homosocial, the world of history departments, like that of the university in general, is heterosocial: our world is no longer exclusively female. For another, the expansion of the field has brought some remarkable innovation. Not only do we now take differences among women to be axiomatic, having heeded the criticism of women of color, of Third World women, and of lesbians in the 1980s, but we also have refined our theory and increasingly substitute gender for women as the object of our inquiry. The scholarship we produce is thus no longer uniquely focused on women as a singular category. And this has meant that the satisfying cohesiveness of the movement—women as subjects and objects of their own history—has disappeared, if indeed it ever existed. I will suggest later that this cohesiveness has largely been established retrospectively, as part of the nostalgia of melancholy.[17]

At one point in their cross-generational exchange,[18] Faue uses an occupational metaphor to characterize the change in the practice of women's history over the past decades. She suggests that a generation of artisans and their apprentices had carefully crafted histories "that had political meaning and sound methodology" (210). They then faced competition from "other historians" who, either less committed to feminism or in possession of "hot theories" (or both), flooded the market with shoddy, mass-produced goods. Although craftswomen continued to produce work of high quality, it was hard to distinguish it from the cheap stuff. As a result, the entire enterprise was devalued. Faue's colleagues reject the metaphor as inapt—Cahn notes that "there was certainly no shortage of 'bad' history produced by the older 'artisanal' mode" (215)—and Faue doesn't insist on it. (A really nice aspect of this conversation, enabled by e-mail technology, is its informality and the willingness of the participants to be tentative, exploratory, and open.) I find the resort to a model of proletarianization telling, not because of its inapplicability to the field of women's history—theories of social movements offer more relevant comparisons than theories of occupational transformation—but because workers in the nineteenth and twentieth centuries and labor historians repeatedly mourn the precapitalist world we have lost. In Faue's use of it, the theme of proletarianization articulates affective loss in more familiar (and more distancing) economic terms. It is, I submit, at least partly the inability to acknowledge directly the affective loss— the passionate idealization of women that drove women's history and historians of women—that makes it, in Faue's words, "so hard to see through the veil that hides the future from the present" (211).

Melancholy

The "veil that hides the future" is Freud's "shadow of the object": melancholy. I take it to mean that we've been confused about the source of our passion, mistaking "women" for the excitement of the new and unknown. What if our sense that we already know what feminist history is blocks the divine madness, the inspired arousal, that is precisely an encounter with the unknown? What if we rewrote feminism's history as the story of a circulating critical passion, slipping metonymically along a chain of contiguous objects, alighting for a while in an unexpected place, accomplishing a task, and then moving on? I use the term "feminism's history" here to mean not only the history of feminism and the history written by feminists, but also as a colloquial insinuation, as in "well, you know, that woman has a history."

At least since the eighteenth century, feminism has used history in different ways and at different times as a critical weapon in the struggle for women's emancipation. Feminism's history has offered demonstrations, in the form of exemplary instances from the past, of women's worthiness to engage in the same activities as men, such as wage earning, education, citizenship, and ruling. It has provided heroines to emulate and lineages for contemporary activists—membership in fictive families of history makers. Feminism's history has exposed as instruments of patriarchal power stories that explained the exclusion of women as a fact of nature. And it has written new histories to counter the lie of women's passivity, as well as their erasure from the records that constitute collective memory. It has not only contested stereotypical versions of woman, it has also insisted on profound differences among women. And it has formed any number of alliances, focused on many aspects of power, to advance its ends. Feminism's history is both a compilation of women's experiences and a record of the different strategic interventions employed to argue women's cause. It can, of course, stand on its own; but it is best understood as a doubly subversive critical engagement, both with prevailing normative codes of gender and with the conventions and—since history's formation as a discipline in the late nineteenth century—rules of historical writing. Feminism's history has been a variable, mutable endeavor, a flexible strategic instrument not bound to any orthodoxy. The production of knowledge about the past, although crucial, has not been an end in itself but rather—at certain moments, and not always in the service of an organized political movement—has provided the substantive terms for a critical operation that uses the past to disrupt the certainties of the present and so opens the way to imagining a different future. This critical operation is the dynamic that drives feminism; in Lacanian terms, it is an operation of desire, unsatisfied by any particular object, "constant in its pressure," ever in search of a fulfillment that is elusive because attaining the utopian aim of abolishing sexual difference altogether would mean the death of feminism.[19]

Desire, Lacan tells us, is driven by lack, ruled by dissatisfaction; it is "unsatisfied, impossible, misconstrued."[20] Its existence exposes the insufficiency of any conclusive settlement; something more is always wanted. Desire moves metonymically; relations among its objects are characterized by unexpected contiguities. The movements are lateral, and they don't follow a single direction. We might say here that for feminism, desire is driven by a form of critique—or, better, is itself a critical faculty. As the German philosophers such as Kant, Hegel, Marx, and the members of the Frankfurt School defined it, critique has the same dissatisfied, unconscious, passionate quality. Although its formulations are rational, its motivations are not entirely known. Wendy Brown and Janet Halley describe critique as "a disruptive, disorienting and at times destructive enterprise of knowledge."[21] They write: "In the insistence on the availability of all human production to critique, that is to the possibility of being rethought through an examination of constitutive premises, the work of critique is potentially without boundary or end" (26). The objects of critique are the forms and manifestations of ideology and power—their underlying truths and foundational assumptions—and these are as varied and unpredictable as desire's objects. As Brown and Halley describe it, critique (like desire) consists in pursuit: "it embodies a will to knowledge" whose exercise yields pleasure—the pleasure that comes from contemplation of the unknown (30). For them, "critique hazards the opening of new modalities of thought and political possibility, and potentially affords as well the possibility of enormous pleasure—political, intellectual, and ethical" (29). The fact that pleasure means not just positive affect but passion is indicated by references to a "kindling spirit," "euphoria," and "pleasure itself as a crucial source of political motivation" (32).

Conceiving of feminism as a restless critical operation, as a movement of desire, detaches it from its origins in Enlightenment teleologies and the utopian promise of complete emancipation. It does not, however, assume that desire operates outside of time; rather, it is a mutating historical phenomenon, defined as and through its displacements. Feminism emerged in the context of liberal democracy's proclamation of universal equality, discursively positioned in and as contradiction—not just in the arena of political citizenship, but in most areas of economic and social life. Despite many changes in the meanings and practices of liberal democracy, its discursive hegemony remains, and feminism is one of its contradictions. By calling attention to itself as contradiction, feminism has challenged the ways in which differences of sex have been used to organize relations of power. Feminism's historical specificity comes from the fact that it works within and against whatever are the prevailing foundational assumptions of its time. Its critical force comes from the fact that it exposes the contradictions in systems that claim to be coherent— such as republicanism that excludes women from citizenship; political economy that attributes women's lower wages to their biologically determined lower value as producers; medical teaching that conflates sexual desire with the natural imperatives of reproduction; and exclusions within women's movements that press for universal emancipation—and calls into question the validity of categories taken as first principles of social organization: *the* family, *the* individual, *the* worker, masculine, feminine, Man, Woman.[22]

One example from our own times of the critical operation of feminism is the relationship of women's history to social history. It is often said, with a certain sense of inevitability, that women's history became acceptable with the rise to prominence of social history. The emphasis on everyday life, ordinary people, and collective action made women an obvious group to include. I would put it differently: there was nothing in social history that made the rise of women's history inevitable. Rather, feminists argued, within the terms and against the grain of behaviorism and new left Marxism, that women were a necessary consideration for social historians. If they were omitted, key insights were lost about the ways class was constructed. While male historians celebrated the democratic impulses of the nascent working class, historians of women pointed to its gender hierarchies. Not only did we correct for the absence of women in labor histories—although we surely did that, showing that "worker" was an exclusionary category; that women were skilled workers, not just a cheap source of labor; and that women called strikes and organized unions, rather than simply being members of the ladies' auxiliary—we also offered a critique of the ways in which labor historians reproduced the machismo of trade unionists. This did not always sit well; indeed, feminists continue to find themselves ghettoized at meetings of labor historians. But there was a certain thrill of discovery as we tried to lead our colleagues to unknown territory. In the process we did convince some of them to consider the ways in which gender consolidated men's identity as workers and as members of a working class, and the ways in which nature was used not only to justify differential treatments of male and female workers, but to regulate family structure and patterns of employment.

In labor history as in other areas of history, from diplomatic to cultural, Faue comments, "women's history has 'defamiliarized' the terrain of other historians."[23] Defamiliarized is exactly right: the meanings taken for granted, the terms by which historians had explained the past, the lists of so-called appropriate topics for historical research were all called into question and shown to be neither as comprehensive nor as objective as had previously been believed. What was once unthinkable—that gender was a useful tool of historical analysis—has become thinkable. But that's not the end of the story. Now a received disciplinary category, gender is being critically examined by the next wave of feminists and others, who rightly insist that it is only one of several equally relevant axes of difference. Sex doesn't subsume race, ethnicity, nationality, or sexuality; these attributions of identity intersect in ways that need to be specified. To restrict our view to sexual difference is thus to miss the always complex ways in which relations of power are signified by *differences*. The newly safe terrain of gender and women's history is now itself being defamiliarized, as queer, postcolonial, and ethnic studies (among other fields) challenge us to push the boundaries of our knowledge, to slide or leap metonymically to contiguous domains. It may seem premature to branch out before we have fully consolidated our gains, but that's the wrong way to think about feminism's history. The impulse to reproduce what is already known is profoundly conservative, whether it comes from traditional political historians or historians of women. What continues to make feminism's history so exciting is precisely its radical refusal to settle down, to call even a comfortable lodging a home.

The Fantasy of Home

Melancholy rests on a fantasy of a home that never really was. Our idealization of the intensely political, woman-oriented moment of recent feminist history and our desire to preserve it, by speaking of it as the essence of women's history, has prevented us from appreciating the excitement and energy of the critical activity that was then and is now the defining characteristic of feminism. Feminist history was never primarily concerned with documenting the experiences of women in the past, even if that was the most visible means by which we pursued our objective. The point of looking to the past was to destabilize the present, to challenge patriarchal institutions and ways of thinking that legitimated themselves as natural, to make the unthinkable thought—for example, to detach gender from sex. In the 1970s and 1980s, women's history was part of a movement that consolidated the identity of women as political subjects, enabling activism in many spheres of society and winning unprecedented public visibility and, eventually, some success. The Equal Rights Amendment did not pass, but other antidiscrimination measures did. Title IX had a tremendous impact, as did affirmative action and campaigns to identify and punish sexual harassment. Patriarchy did not fall, gender hierarchies remain, and backlash is evident (evolutionary psychology is its most recent incarnation), but many barriers to women—especially to white, middle-class, professional women—have been removed. And the United Nations has called for the entire world to acknowledge that women's rights are human rights. Women's status as subjects of history, subject producers of historical knowledge, and subjects of politics seems to have been secured, in principle if not always in practice.

The public acceptance of women's identity as political subjects made the historical construction of that identity redundant; there was nothing new to be championed in this realm. Stories designed to celebrate women's agency began to seem predictable and repetitious, just more information garnered to prove a point that had already been made. Moreover, the politics of identity took a melancholic, conservative turn in the last decades of the twentieth century, as Wendy Brown has so persuasively demonstrated.[24] Victims and their injuries came to the fore and, though a good deal of effort was expended on their behalf, the situation of women as wounded subjects does not inspire either creative politics or history. Increasingly, too, differences among women became more difficult to reconcile in a single category, even if it was pluralized. "Women," however modified, seemed too much a universalization of white, Western, straight women—a category not capacious enough to alone do the work that considerations of differences among women required. The emergence of new political movements seemed to call for new kinds of political subjects; singular identities no longer worked as they once had for the construction of multiple and mutable strategic alliances. In this context, a new generation of feminists turned their critical lens on the construction of identity itself as a historical process. Seeking to defamiliarize identity's contemporary claims, they emphasized the complex ways in which the identity of "women" operates, not just to signify gender. If race, sexuality, ethnicity, and nationality play equally significant parts in the definition of "women," then gender is not a useful enough category of analysis.

But to tell the story in the way that I have implies a singular narrative, which distorts the past. We didn't move neatly from identity to gender to a critique of subject formation. Feminism's history in these years is not a story of a unified assault: Clio brandishing gender and singing of women. Even as the identity of women was being consolidated, even as women seemed the primary object of our inquiry, there were critical, conflicting voices pointing out the limits of women and gender as concepts, introducing other objects and theorizing different ways of considering the historical significances of sexual difference. In 1975 Gayle Rubin opened the way for (among other things) the rethinking and historicizing of normative heterosexuality.[25] In 1976 Natalie Davis cautioned us to study not women but gender groups, and she refused reductive readings of the symbols of masculine and feminine, reminding us of the multiple and complex historical meanings of those categories.[26] In 1982 the ninth Barnard Conference on the Scholar and the Feminist was blown apart by debates about the place of sex in representations of women's agency.[27] In 1988 Denise Riley suggested that the category of women was not foundational, but historical.[28] In 1989 Ann Snitow pointed out that feminism was divided by irreconcilable desires for both sameness and difference.[29] In 1992 Evelyn Brooks Higginbotham, hoping to escape the totalizing effects of simple oppositions between white and black women, theorized about "the metalanguage of race." "By fully recognizing race as an unstable, shifting, and strategic reconstruction," she wrote, "feminist scholars must take up new challenges to inform and confound many of the assumptions currently underlying Afro-American history and women's history. We must problematize much more of what we take for granted. We must bring to light and to coherence the one and the many that we always were in history and still actually are today."[30] And in 1997 Afsaneh Najmabadi declared her "not-so-hidden pleasure at being unable or unwilling to identify myself in [recognizable identity terms] no matter how many times hybridized" and also confounded those terms in her work on gender and nation building in Iran.[31]

I offer these examples with dates attached not to demonstrate a cumulative process through which our work got smarter or more sophisticated. Precisely the opposite is the case. The critical questioning of prevailing categories both of mainstream and of feminist work is consistently present, and its object keeps changing; these examples are illustrations of the metonymic slippage I referred to above. In fact, in a riot of promiscuous exploration (Faue's "wild cacophony"), many objects overlap and coexist, including sexuality, race, symbols of masculine and feminine, the changing representation and uses of gender and racial difference, and the intersections of race, ethnicity, and gender in nation building. It is this critical activity—the relentless interrogation of the taken-for-granted—that always moves us somewhere else, from object to object, from the present to the future. Those accounts that insist that women are, have been, and must ever be the sole subject or object of feminist history tell a highly selective story that obscures the dynamic that makes thinking the future possible. Of course there have been strenuous efforts at boundary keeping, and these selective stories are among them, but they have been of little avail: heedless of the broken hearts left in its wake, feminist critical desire keeps moving. This is not a betrayal or a defection, but a triumph; it is the way the passion of the feminist critical spirit is kept alive.

Identity

I have been arguing that the primary role of feminist history has been not to produce women as subjects, but to explore and contest the means and effects of that subject production as it has varied over time and circumstance. To rest content with any identity—even one we have helped produce—is to give up the work of critique. That goes for our identity both as historians and as feminists: having won entry into the profession by exposing its politics of disciplinary formation, it won't do now to settle down and enforce the existing rules, even if we have helped create some of them. It's not a matter of an anarchic refusal of discipline, but a subversive use of its methods and a more self-conscious willingness to entertain topics and approaches that were once considered out of bounds. It's what we don't know that entices us; it's new stories that we yearn to tell, new memories that we seek to reveal. Our passion for women's history was a desire to know and think what had hitherto been unthinkable. Passion, after all, thrives on the pursuit of the not-yet-known.

Interdisciplinarity has been one of the ways we have learned to tell new stories. That's why it has been a hallmark of feminist scholarship. Women's studies seminars, programs, and departments have been the proving grounds for the articulation of new knowledge. They have provided sustenance for research considered untenable in traditional departments, legitimation for those who might otherwise have been untenurable. It was questions posed from outside our own disciplinary problematic that often prodded historians such as myself to seek unconventional answers; it was the engaged response from other feminist scholars that made the work seem worthwhile. The call of other muses supplemented Clio's inspiration. We had at least two things in common: questions about women, gender, and power and—

because simply comparing data about women didn't get us very far—a quest for theories that could provide alternative ways of seeing and knowing. "Theory," Stuart Hall has famously stated, "makes meanings slide."[32] And it was exactly that destabilization of received meaning that was feminism's aim. The exploration of theory—including Marxism, psychoanalysis, liberalism, structuralism, and poststructuralism—and the attempt to formulate something we could call feminist theory were ways of overcoming disciplinary barriers, finding a common language despite our different academic formations. Although many historians of women, echoing their disciplinary colleagues, worried that theory and history were incompatible, in fact it was theory that enabled the critique of a history that assumed a singular knowing subject (*the* historian) and considered some topics more worthy of investigation than others. Whether or not it is now widely acknowledged, some commonly accepted axioms of feminist historical analysis are in fact theoretical insights about how differences are constructed: there is neither a self nor a collective identity without an Other (or others); there is no inclusiveness without exclusion, no universal without a rejected particular, no neutrality that doesn't privilege an interested point of view; and power is always at issue in the articulation of these relationships. Taken as analytic points of departure, these axioms have become the foundation of an ongoing and far-reaching critical historical inquiry.

Feminist history thrives on interdisciplinary encounters and has incorporated some of the teachings of theory, but it has rightly considered its primary focus to be the discipline of history itself. (After all, it's Clio who turns us on.) The tension between feminism and history, between subversion and establishment, has been difficult and productive; the one pushing the limits of orthodoxy, the other policing the boundaries of acceptable knowledge. Whether or not we know it, the relationship is not one-sided but interdependent. Feminism transforms the discipline by critically addressing its problematic from the perspective of gender and power, but without the disciplinary problematic there would be no feminist history. Since the problematic changes (only partly because feminism transforms it), feminist history changes as well. After all, memory is not static, nor is Clio's inspiration. Feminism's history is always articulated in critical relation to the discipline of history. Where is the feminist critique of cultural history? Of rationalist interpretations of behavior? What are the limits of now-accepted disciplinary understandings of gender? What are the histories of the uses of the categories of difference— racial, sexual, religious, ethnic, national, and so on—that historians take to be self-evident characterizations of people in the past? These questions, relentless interrogations of accepted knowledges and approaches to them, are the signs of an active, future-oriented feminist critical desire.[33]

If we relate to our discipline as a kind of critical gadfly, we do the same to our colleagues in other disciplines and in newer areas of interdisciplinary study. It is we who introduce the difference of time into the categories employed by queer, postcolonial, transnational, and global studies. Strategic affiliations aren't without their critical dimensions; feminist historians specialize in the temporal dimension. We're relativists when it comes to meanings; we know they vary over time. That makes us particularly good cultural critics. We can historicize the present's fundamental truths and expose the kinds of investments that drive them, in this way using the past not as the precursor to what is (typically the task of official history), but as its foil. Here we are double agents, practicing history to deepen and sharpen the critiques of new oppositional studies, while slyly repudiating the discipline's emphasis on continuity and the unidirectionality of causality, from past to present. There's a great future for double agents of this kind and a certain thrill in the job. It's destabilizing both to those we engage with and to ourselves. There's no worry that our identity will become fixed, or our work complacent; there are always new strategic decisions to be made. To be sure, there are risks involved when orthodoxies on the Left and the Right are challenged. But those are the risks that have characterized feminism's history from the beginning, the source of both pleasure and danger, the guarantee of an opening to the future. Inderpal Grewal, Caren Kaplan, and Robyn Wiegman call their series of feminist scholarship at Duke University Press Next Wave Provocations, suggesting that there's no end to feminism's history—the passionate pursuit of the not-yet-known.[34]

Critique

"Ah, the future"—it is perilous only if one denies feminist agency. Feminists are not only political subjects but also desiring subjects and, as such, subjects who make history. This notion of agency as impelled by a quest for what we cannot ultimately know—by desire— is not mine, nor is it new. In 1983 Ann Snitow, Christine Stansell, and Sharon Thompson edited a book of essays called *The Powers of Desire: The Politics of Sexuality*.[35] Its major points are that women are not only political beings but also sexual beings and that the study of sexuality—from many perspectives—opens up "an area for play, for experimentation." The editors also associate feminist scholarship with desire; and "desire," they write, pointing to a distant horizon where "we might see what is coming in our direction," "is ever renewed" (43). I have extended this argument beyond the topic of sex and sexuality to characterize feminist agency itself. Our agency—our desire—is critique, the constant undoing of conventional wisdom; the exposure of its limits for fully satisfying the goals of equality. It drives us to unforeseen places. You never know what will next draw our attention or our ire. Critique, as desire, provides no map. It is rather a standard against which to measure the dissatisfactions of the present. Its path can be seen only in retrospect, but its motion is undeniable.[36] Historical study is a particularly effective form of feminist critique.

Some ancient representations of Clio show her with a trumpet and a clepsydra (a water clock), perhaps heralding the passage of time. Time conceived as fluidity or flow—a particularly feminine representation—is not easily contained. Clio is also shown with writing implements, books, and scrolls, referring to the fact that she introduced the Phoenician alphabet to the Greeks. If Clio offered the tools of knowledge production, our task is to use them. We are not gods and thus cannot, like her, tell true tales, so we are driven by our critical faculty—which she inspires and arouses—always to revise, always to reach beyond our grasp for new knowledge, new stories to tell.

Since Clio has from the beginning been our inspiration, it's important to learn some things about her that aren't so well known. The muses had no permanent home: they danced on Mount Olympus, but Mount Helicon was also their haunt. And they did not sit or walk, they flew: "Wherever they go they may go flying; for in such a way goddesses usually travel, as King Pyreneus of Daulis, who attempted to rape them, too late learned. For he perished when he leapt from the pinnacle of a tower trying to follow the flying Muses who escaped him."[37] Those who fly escape the dangers of domination, the tyrannical powers of orthodoxy. Flight is also a positive course, a soaring; it traces the path of desire. When melancholy is left behind, that path opens for us. And passion returns as it readies itself for its latest pursuit of what has not yet been thought.

2. Fantasy Echo

History and the Construction of Identity

THE TITLE OF THIS CHAPTER is not a technical term. In origin it was a mistake, the result of a student's inability to understand some French words spoken in heavily accented English by a German-born professor of history. The student, who also had no familiarity with some of the grand themes of modern European intellectual history, tried to capture the sounds he had heard and render them phonetically, echoing imperfectly, though not unrecognizably, the professor's reference to the designation by contemporaries of the last decades of the nineteenth century as the *fin de siècle*. There were enough clues in the student's final exam for me eventually to figure out what he meant. (I was a teaching assistant for George Mosse at the University of Wisconsin then—it was 1964 or 1965). There was something about the student's choice of words that appealed to me—perhaps their sheer linguistic creativity or perhaps the fact that they could be construed to have a certain descriptive plausibility. In any case, I never forgot them. Now, in the wake of our own *fin de siècle*, the words "fantasy echo" seem to have extraordinary resonance, offering a way of thinking not only about the significance of arbitrary temporal designations (decades, centuries, millennia) but also about how we appeal to and write history. Although I have no idea who the student was who coined the phrase (and I would bet that he has long since forgotten his desperate improvisation), it might be that "fantasy echo" could become one of those clever formulations that also does useful interpretive work.

Identity and History

For a while I have been writing critically about identity, insisting that identities don't preexist their strategic political invocations, that categories of identity we take for granted as rooted in our physical bodies (gender and race) or our cultural (ethnic, religious) heritages are, in fact, retrospectively linked to those roots; they don't follow predictably or naturally from them.[1] There's an illusory sameness established by referring to a category of person (women, workers, African Americans, homosexuals) as if it never changed, as if not the category, but only its historical circumstances, varied over time. Thus women's historians (to take the example I know best) have asked how changes in the legal, social, economic, and medical status of women affected their possibilities for emancipation or equality; but they have asked less often how these changes altered the meaning (socially articulated, subjectively understood) of the term "women" itself. Few feminist historians (Denise Riley is the exception here) have heeded the advice of Michel Foucault to historicize the categories that the present takes to be self-evident realities.[2] Even though, for Foucault, the "history of the present" served a clear political end (denaturalizing the categories on which contemporary structures of power rested and so destabilizing those structures of power), those who resist his teaching have taken historicization to be synonymous with depoliticization. This synonymity is only true, however, if historical rootedness is seen as a prerequisite for the stability of the subject of feminism, if the existence of feminism is made to depend on some inherent, timeless agency of women.

While historians have been quick to acknowledge Eric Hobsbawm's reminder that tradition is an "invention" that serves to inspire and legitimize contemporary political action by finding precedents and inspiration for it in the past, they have been slow to apply this idea to categories of identity—or at least to categories of identity that have physical or cultural referents.[3] Hobsbawm's writing on this topic came as part of the reassessment of Marxist (or, more accurately, Stalinist) historiography, with its ahistoric notions of workers and class struggle, and it had an important influence on the historicizing of those concepts (there has been little work, though, among labor historians on the question of how the "invention of tradition" operates). In the field of women's history Hobsbawm's intervention has been largely ignored; there, an increasing number of histories of feminism are producing continuous histories of women's activism, heedless, it would seem, of their own inventions. This may be a result of the fact that it is harder to historicize the category of women, based as it seems to be in biology, than it was to historicize the category of worker, always understood to be a social phenomenon, produced not by nature, but by economic and political arrangements. It may also stem from the greater difficulty those who write about women (as opposed to workers) have had in dispelling stereotypes about women's apolitical natures and their consequent lack of political participation. Thus there exists the temptation to pile up counterexamples as demonstrations of women's political capacity and to neglect the changing, and often radically different, historical contexts within which women as subjects came into being.

But even those who grant that collective identities are invented as part of some effort of political mobilization haven't attended to how the process of invention works. In *Only Paradoxes to Offer*, I tried, in the last section of each of the biographical chapters, to demonstrate that feminist identity was an effect of a rhetorical political strategy invoked differently by different feminists at different times.[4] These sections constitute a critique of the notion that the history of feminism, or for that matter the history of women, is continuous. I offer instead a story of discontinuity that was repeatedly sutured by feminist activists in the eighteenth and nineteenth centuries into a vision of uninterrupted linear succession: women's activism on behalf of women. The identity of women, I argue, was not so much a self-evident fact of history as it was evidence—from particular and discrete moments in time—of someone's, some group's, effort to identify and thereby mobilize a collectivity.

The argument I advanced in those chapter sections constituted for me a way of pursuing Foucault's genealogical agenda of critically intervening in disciplinary debates about identity and the writing of history. But it also left aside questions about how identity was established, how women with vastly different agendas identified with one another across time and social positions. What were the mechanisms of such collective and retrospective identification? How do these mechanisms operate? In looking for ways to answer these questions I am tempted to try to make fantasy echo do serious analytic work.

Fantasy

"Fantasy echo" has a wonderfully complex resonance. Depending on whether the words are both taken as nouns or as an adjective and a noun, the term signifies the repetition of something imagined or an imagined repetition. In either case the repetition is not exact, since an echo is an imperfect return of sound. Fantasy, as noun or adjective, refers to plays of the mind that are creative and not always rational. For thinking the problem of retrospective identification it may not matter which is the noun and which the adjective. Retrospective identifications, after all, are imagined repetitions and repetitions of imagined resemblances. The echo is a fantasy, the fantasy an echo; the two are inextricably intertwined. What might it mean to characterize the operations of retrospective identification as a fantasized echo or an echoed fantasy? It might mean simply that such identification is established by the finding of resemblances between actors present and past. There is no shortage of writing about history in these terms: history as the result of empathetic identification made possible either by the existence of universal human characteristics or, in some instances, by a transcendent set of traits and experiences belonging to women or workers or members of religious or ethnic communities. In this view of things, fantasy is the means by which real relations of identity between past and present are discovered and/or forged. Fantasy is more or less synonymous with imagination, and it is taken to be subject to rational, intentional control; one directs one's imagination purposively to achieve a coherent aim, that of writing oneself or one's group into history, writing the history of individuals or groups.[5] The limits of this approach for my purposes are that it assumes exactly the continuity—the essentialist nature—of identity that I want to question.

For that reason I have turned to writings, informed by psychoanalysis, that treat fantasy in its unconscious dimensions. Substantively, it may be that certain shared fantasies—the ones Jean Laplanche and Jean-Bertrand Pontalis deem "primal fantasies"—provide fundamental terms for sexed identities. These fantasies are the myths cultures develop to answer questions about the origins of subjects, sexual difference, and sexuality.[6] Primal fantasies of sexual difference (which assume the female body has been castrated) may provide a ground of unconscious commonality among women who are otherwise historically and socially different. But this can't account either for the subjectively different perceptions women have of themselves as women or for the ways in which at certain moments "women" become consolidated as an identity group. I want to argue that the commonality among women does not preexist its invocation but rather that it is secured by fantasies that enable them to transcend history and difference.

It seems more useful, therefore, to consider fantasy as a formal mechanism for the articulation of scenarios that are at once historically specific in their representation and detail and transcendent of historical specificity. There are three aspects of fantasy (not all of which are necessary characteristics) that are useful for my purposes. The first is that fantasy is the setting for desire. "Fantasy," write Laplanche and Pontalis, "is not the object of desire, but its setting. In fantasy the subject does not pursue the object or its sign: he appears caught up himself in the sequence of images. He forms no representation of the desired object, but is himself represented as participating in the scene."[7] In the fantasized setting the fulfillment of desire and the consequences of this fulfillment are enacted. "Fantasy" Riley defines as "sustained metaphoricity. To be in fantasy is to live 'as if.' Some scene is being played out; and any act of identification necessarily entails a scenario."[8] The second formal aspect is that fantasy has a double structure, which at once reproduces and masks conflict, antagonism, or contradiction. In Freud's classic essay "A Child Is Being Beaten," fantasy simultaneously enacts the individual's transgressive wish and punishes the wisher. The beating is both the fulfillment of the child's erotic desire for the father and punishment for it.[9]

In Slavoj Žižek's analysis of ideology, filtered through a Lacanian lens, fantasy maintains and masks divisions within society. It does so in some instances by attributing to reviled others (Jews are one classic example) the causes of one's own (or a group's) lack of satisfaction: "they" have stolen "our" *jouissance*. The we-versus-they construction consolidates each side as an undifferentiated whole and effaces the differences that produce hierarchy and conflict among "us"; it also articulates a longing for enjoyment that it is beyond the ability of any ideological system to provide. (Jouissance is crucial in Žižek's discussion of fantasy; it is that orgasmic sensation that exceeds articulation and seems, momentarily at least, to satisfy desire. But desire is ultimately unsatisfiable since it seeks to restore an imagined wholeness and coherence, the end of the alienation associated with the acquisition of individual selfhood.) In another of Žižek's instances, fantasy contains the libidinal "obscene supplement" on which power is based —the underlying and usually unstated erotic appeal of, say, antipornography legislation that depicts exactly what it aims to regulate and/or repress.[10] A third formal aspect is that fantasy operates as a (tightly condensed) narrative. In Žižek's formulation, the narrative is a way of resolving "some fundamental antagonism by rearranging its terms into a temporal succession" (11). Contradictory elements (or, for that matter, incoherent ones) are rearranged diachronically, becoming causes and effects. Instead of desire/punishment or transgression/law being seen as mutually constitutive, they are understood to operate sequentially: the transgressions of desire bring about the law's punishment or, to change the example, the advent of modernity brings the "loss" of traditional society. In fact, the qualities said to belong to traditional society come into existence only with the emergence of modernity; they are its constitutive underside. The relationship is not diachronic but synchronic. Thus the imposition of narrative logic on history is itself a fantasy according to Žižek: "Actual historical breaks are, if anything, more radical than mere narrative deployments, since what changes in them is the entire constellation of emergence and loss. In other words, a true historical break does not simply designate the 'regressive' loss (or 'progressive' gain) of something, but the shift in the very grid which enables us to measure losses and gains" (13).

Fantasy is at play in the articulation of both individual and collective identity; it extracts coherence from confusion, reduces multiplicity to singularity, and reconciles illicit desire with the law. It enables individuals and groups to give themselves histories. "Fantasy," writes Jacqueline Rose, "is not . . . antagonistic to social reality; it is its precondition or psychic glue."[11] Fantasy can help account for the ways subjects are formed, internalizing and resisting social norms, taking on the terms of identity that endow them with agency. (For that reason it has informed both pessimistic and optimistic theories about human subjectivity.)[12] And it can be used to study the ways in which history—a fantasized narrative that imposes sequential order on otherwise chaotic and contingent occurrences—contributes to the articulation of political identity. Thus, as I have argued elsewhere, the history of feminism, when told as a continuous, progressive story of women's quest for emancipation, effaces the discontinuity, conflict, and difference that might undermine the politically desired stability of the categories termed "women" and "feminist."[13]

In fantasy, narrative operations are not straightforward, precisely because of the condensed way in which temporality is figured. There is always a certain ambiguity created by the coexistence of simultaneity and narrative. In the fantasy scenario, desire is fulfilled, punished, and prohibited all at once, in the same way that social antagonism is evoked, erased, and resolved. But the fantasy also implies a story about a sequential relationship for prohibition, fulfillment, and punishment (having broken the law that prohibits incest, the child is being beaten); and it is precisely narrative that evokes, erases, and thereby resolves social antagonism ("we" are responding to "others" who have taken away our jouissance). The sequence of events in the scenario substitutes (or stands in) for historical change (which, I would argue, is about the existence of difference in time). Repetition replaces history (or is conflated with it) because the narrative is already contained in the scenario. Writing oneself into the story being staged thus becomes a way of writing oneself into history. In this way the category of identity is retrospectively stabilized. What might be called the fantasy of feminist history secures the identity of women over time. The particular details may be different, but the repetition of the basic narrative and the subject's experience in it means that the actors are known to us—they are us.

Still, there is a tension to be explored by historians seeking to analyze processes of identity formation, a tension between the temporality of historical narrative (which carries with it notions of irreducible difference in time) and its condensation in recurring scenarios (which seem to deny that difference). That is where echo comes in.

Echo

In its most literal sense echo simply repeats what came before, multiplying copies, prolonging the sound—identity as reproduction of the same. But this literalness isn't even right as a description of the physical phenomenon. Echoes are delayed returns of sound; they are incomplete reproductions, usually giving back only the final fragments of a phrase. An echo spans large gaps of space (sound reverberates between distant points) and time (echoes are not instantaneous), but it also creates gaps of meaning and intelligibility. The melodic tolling of bells can become cacophonous when echoes mingle with the original sound; when the sounds are words, the return of partial phrases alters the original sense and comments on it as well. Poets and literary scholars have made much of this incomplete, belated, and often contradictory kind of repetition. In one translator's rendition of Ovid's story of Echo and Narcissus, where Echo's effect is to transform others' meaning, Narcissus cries, "Here let us meet, let us come together," and she replies (turning his search for the source of the voice he hears into her erotic proposition), "Let us come. Together."[14] Or, when Narcissus recoils from Echo's embrace and says, "may I die before I give you power over me," she responds, "I give you power over me," reversing the pronoun's referent and the import of the words.[15] Here an echo provides ironic contrast; in other instances an echo's mimicry creates a mocking effect. In either case, repetition constitutes alteration. It is thus that echo undermines the notion of enduring sameness that often attaches to identity. Claire Nouvet reads the story of Echo and Narcissus as a commentary on the way subjects are constructed. When, rejected by Narcissus, Echo loses her body, Ovid tells us that she nonetheless remains alive as sound ("There is sound, which lives in her").[16]

> Although Echo is now a sound, the text still posits her as a subject capable of containing a sound. But since Echo has lost her body, since there is "no-

body" left, how can the sound be in her? The disembodiment "kills" Echo, the "other," by exposing the subjective other as the deceptive embodiment of an echoing Other. (114)

Echo, in Nouvet's reading, is the process by which subjects come into being as "a play of repetition and difference among signifiers" (114).[17] This emphasis on language is no doubt important, but it is also limited for thinking about the historical processes involved in the formation of identity. It is precisely by filling the empty categories of self and other with recognizable representatives that fantasy works to secure identity. In my use of it, echo is not so much a symptom of the empty, illusory nature of otherness as it is a reminder of the temporal inexactness of fantasy's condensations, condensations that nonetheless work to conceal or minimize difference through repetition. (Inexact usages of echo capture this occluding operation when they imply that echo is an exact replication of the original sound.)

For historians, echo provides yet another take on the process of establishing identity by raising the issues of the distinction between the original sound and its resonances and the role of time in the distortions heard. Where does an identity originate? Does the sound issue forth from past to present, or do answering calls echo to the present from the past? If we are not the source of the sound, how can we locate that source? If all we have is the echo, can we ever discern the original? Is there any point in trying, or can we be content with thinking about identity as a series of repeated transformations?

The historian who writes about women participates in this echo effect, sending forth and picking up sounds. Women, as a designated topic of research, is a plural noun signifying differences among biological females; it is also a collective term that occludes differences among women, usually by contrasting them with men. Women's history implies smooth continuity, but also divisions and differences. Indeed, the distinctive word "women" refers to so many subjects, different and the same, that the word becomes a series of fragmented sounds, rendered intelligible only by the listener, who (in specifying her object) is predisposed to listen in a certain way. "Women" acquires intelligibility when the historian or the activist looking for inspiration from the past attributes significance to (identifies with) what she has been able to hear. If the historically defined subjectivity that is identity is thought of as an echo, then replication is no longer an apt synonym. Identity as a continuous, coherent, historical phenomenon is revealed to be a fantasy, a fantasy that erases the divisions and discontinuities, the absences and differences, that separate subjects in time. Echo provides a gloss on fantasy and destabilizes any effort to limit the possibilities of "sustained metaphoricity" by reminding us that identity (in the sense both of sameness and selfness) is constructed in complex and diffracted relation to others. Identification (which produces identity) operates as a fantasy echo, then, replaying in time and over generations the process that forms individuals as social and political actors.

Two Fantasies of Feminist History

Although many fantasies have been produced to consolidate feminist identity, two seem to me particularly prevalent, at least in Western feminist movements since the late eighteenth century. One, the fantasy of the female orator, projects women into masculine public space, where they experience the pleasures and dangers of transgressing social and sexual boundaries. The other, the feminist maternal fantasy, seems at first to be contrary to the orator in its acceptance of rules that define reproduction as women's primary role (an acceptance of the difference the equality-seeking orator refuses). But the fantasy, in fact, envisions the end of difference, the recovery of "a lost territory" and the end of the divisiveness, conflict, and alienation associated with individuation.[18] It is a utopian fantasy of sameness and harmony produced by maternal love.

These fantasy scenarios are not permanent fixtures of feminist movements, nor does the use of one preclude an appeal to the other. In fact, in the examples I cite below, the same woman places herself at different moments in each scenario. (This may be because they are related fantasies, the one seeking separation from, the other a return to, the mother.)[19] The fantasies function as resources to be invoked. Indeed, they might be said to have the quality of echoes, resonating incompletely and sporadically, though discernibly, in the appeal to women to identify as feminists.

Orators

In the annals of the history of feminism, one iconic figure is that of a woman standing at a podium giving a speech. The scenario is similar whether the depiction is reverent or caricatured: the woman's arm is raised, she's talking to a crowd, their response is tempestuous, things might be out of control. The tumult acknowledges the transgressive nature of the scene, since in the nineteenth and early twentieth centuries women were excluded, by social convention if not law, from speaking in public forums. The scene itself might be read as a trope for feminism more generally: an exciting—in all the senses of that word—intervention in the (masculine) public, political realm.

In French feminist history the primal scene was staged by Olympe de Gouges: "If women have the right to mount to the scaffold, they ought equally to have the right to mount to the rostrum."[20] Gouges's fate—execution by the Jacobins in 1793—linked the possibility of punishment by death to women's demands for political rights and their exercise of a public voice (substituting for her logical argument a story of transgression and its subsequent punishment). Her own experience with public speaking was not remarkable, and it rarely seems to have literally approximated the fantasized scenario that echoed down the generations of feminist militancy. It is reported that she unsuccessfully tried several times to gain the podium in the National Assembly in the early 1790s and that she addressed a largely female audience at a meeting of the Society of Revolutionary Republican Women in 1793. Gouges's most noted interventions were her voluminous writings, especially her *Declaration of the Rights of Woman and Citizen* of 1791. Of course, writing is also an exercise of public voice, and it was for Gouges a source of enormous pleasure (she had, she once said, "an itch [*démangeaison*] to write").[21] Moreover, Gouges saw nothing transgressive in her own public activity because she did not accept the gendered boundaries of public and private (politics and sex, reason and emotion) that the revolutionaries were implementing, nor did she seek to remove sex from political consideration. Women needed freedom of speech so they could identify the fathers of the children who resulted from sexual encounters, she argued in her *Declaration of the Rights*. The revolution could use women, she pointed out elsewhere, to "inflame the passions" of young men being recruited for the army. The Jacobins, however, defined her actions as inversions of nature and, when they guillotined her, they explained that she had "forgotten the virtues that belong to her sex."[22] It was in this way that Gouges's words about the scaffold and the tribune became the caption for a feminist scenario enacted by succeeding generations.

When Jeanne Deroin campaigned as a democratic socialist for a seat in the legislature in 1849 (despite the fact that women could neither vote nor run for office under the rules of the Second Republic), she told the readers of her newspaper, *L'Opinion des Femmes*, that her speech (to a crowd of mostly male workers) had met with "kind reception." Yet her deep conviction that equality between the sexes was the foundation of socialism was not enough, she confided, to prevent her being overtaken in the course of her speech by "*une vive émotion*," which she feared might have weakened the development of her ideas and the force of her expression. Indeed, for a moment these feelings of pleasure and danger caused her to lose her voice. At another meeting the circumstances were different. As she ascended to the lectern, "a violent uproar burst forth, at first toward the entrance to the hall, and soon the entire assembly joined in." Though fearful, Deroin held her ground (imagining herself, I imagine, to be Gouges) and derived great satisfaction from it: "fortified by the intimate sentiment of the grandeur of our mission, of the holiness of our apostleship and profoundly convinced of the importance . . . of our work, so eminently, so radically revolutionary . . . we accomplished our duty by refusing to leave the tribune . . . to appease the tumultuous crowd."[23] Later Deroin explained that "she was excited [*excitée*] by a powerful impulse [*une impulsion puissante*]" that overcame her natural timidity.[24] Although she attributed this impulse to external influences and explained her action as the performance of duty in the service of a cause, there seems little doubt to me that the excitement experienced in both scenes is that jouissance evoked by Žižek—the excess of pleasure associated with the fulfillment of an illicit wish and its punishment, a punishment that confirms the transgressive nature of the desire.

Madeleine Pelletier (psychiatrist, socialist, suffragist) provides a version of the scene in her autobiographical novel of 1933. The protagonist (dressed, like Pelletier, *en homme* in pants, a collar and tie, with short cropped hair) nervously takes the podium and forcefully urges a hooting crowd of male socialist workers to support women's rights. (The pleasure at assuming the male position is enhanced and offset by fear.) When she's later told by sympathetic comrades that she'd be more effective if she dressed appropriately—as a woman— her reaction to "these brutal words" is shock: "It felt like a sort of moral rape."[25] The clothing of the speaker and the fact that she is speaking signal her inappropriate femininity, which is punished by disapproval so strong that it feels like rape. The violation of normative standards of gender—for Madeleine Pelletier, the joyful ability to transcend the limits of sexual difference—brings violation in its turn, a violation that restores gender boundaries.

There is no doubt that Pelletier had read Deroin's accounts of her experience, as there is little doubt that Deroin had Gouges in mind. Pelletier, in fact, had given her protagonist the nom de guerre of Jeanne Deroin, though Deroin's notions of womanhood and feminism were radically different from her own. Moreover, Gouges, whose formulation became a cherished slogan of French feminism, was a courtesan, a playwright, and of uncertain political sympathies (she was a monarchist until the king's execution in 1792, when she switched her loyalties to the Gironde and federalism). Opinionated, seductive, verbose, she was not at all the woman—whose chaste maternity was exemplified by the Virgin Mary—that Deroin sought to embody in the mid-nineteenth century with a gentle loving demeanor, or the *femme en homme*, striding to the podium, that Pelletier enacted in the early twentieth century. These details—of great importance for the historicizing of identity in general and of women and feminists in particular—were incidental to the collective identification enabled by the fantasy scenario. Indeed, one of the ways in which feminism acquired a history was that successive generations of women (activists and historians) were able to write themselves into these similarly structured scenarios. It was the shared jouissance, not the specific historical details, that provided common ground.

Another version, one that shows the international reach of these fantasy echoes, comes from the German socialist and feminist Lily Braun, who worked in a political, national, and social context very different from the French. "It is so very hard to develop my innermost thoughts in front of strangers,—it is as if I had to show myself naked to the whole world."[26] Nakedness—the exposure of femininity—is at once pleasurably triumphant (her mere presence says: look, there's no mistaking it, a female in male space) and erotically provocative (undermining the feminist effort to deny the importance of sexual difference). A variation of this scenario comes from the psychoanalyst Joan Rivière describing in a 1927 article one of her patients, an accomplished professional and public speaker who, after an impressive performance at the podium regularly abjected herself by flirting with older men in the audience. "All her life," Rivière wrote, "a certain degree of anxiety, sometimes very severe, was experienced after every public performance, such as speaking to an audience. In spite of her unquestionable success and ability, both intellectual and practical, and her capacity for managing an audience and dealing with discussions, etc., she would be excited and apprehensive all night after, with misgivings whether she had done anything inappropriate, and obsessed by a need for reassurance."[27]

By masquerading as a woman, Rivière's patient sought to deny the castrating effects of the impressive and, for her, exciting display of her intellect. The details of Rivière's fantasy reverse Braun's: while Braun imagines herself exposed as an imposter who only pretends to have the phallus, Rivière's patient wants to disguise her possession of the phallus and the pleasure it gives her by donning the mask of "womanliness." But in both of these cases the fantasy permits the evocation and containment of pleasurable excess associated with breaching the boundaries of sexual difference.

The contemporary feminist historian, herself grappling with the joys and anxieties of exercising a public voice, easily reads herself into these scenarios even though good historical sense warns that important differences are being ignored. There is Gouges, whose eighteenth-century aristocratic pretensions included glorying in her sexuality; Deroin, democratic socialist of the 1840s, who adored the idea of maternal chastity; Pelletier, psychiatrist and anarchist at the end of the nineteenth century, deriving erotic pleasure from passing as a man; and Rivière's patient, one of the New Women of the 1920s, unable to resolve an apparent conflict between her professional and sexual identities. In all these instances the

very notions of sex and sexuality—to say nothing of women and feminist—are different, and it behooves the historian of women and feminism to point this out. Yet there is also no denying the persistent fact of
identification, for echoing through the turns and twists of history is the
fantasy scenario: if woman has the right to mount to the scaffold, she has
also the right to mount to the rostrum. It is in the transgression of the
law, of historically and culturally specific regulatory norms, that one
becomes a subject of the law, and it is the excitement at the possibility of
entering this scenario of transgression and fulfillment that provides
continuity for an otherwise discontinuous movement.

Mothers

The woman as mother is the antithesis of the female public speaker.
While the orator wrestles with her inappropriate masculinity, the
mother embodies acceptable femininity, fulfilling as she does her
designated reproductive role. Despite its apparent endorsement of
normative gender relations, maternity has sometimes served to consolidate feminist identification. (Of course, hostility to maternity has
also united feminists, sometimes at the same time, sometimes at
different moments from the positive identification I will describe
here.) Appealing to prevailing ideas of maternity, often in contexts of
pronatalist political pressure, feminists have argued that mothers de-
serve rights because they guarantee the future of the race or the
nation or the species. In these strategic interventions the incentive for
collective mobilization has often rested on the physical sameness of
women's (reproductive) bodies. Gouges spoke in the name of "the
sex superior in beauty as in courage during childbirth" when she
delivered her *Declaration of the Rights of Woman and Citizen.* Deroin
equated womanhood with an idealized mother, one overflowing with
selfless love: "Women are the mothers of humanity, the most important of all work is the production of the human being."[28] And some of
the organizers of the most powerful international feminist networks
at the dawn of the twentieth century used maternity as the common
ground for their antiwar movement. French delegate Maria Verone
called for unity at the International Council of Women meeting in
Rome in May 1914 by appealing "to all women of all nations, who

suffer childbirth with the same pain and who, when their sons die in war, shed the same tears."[29]

There has been much debate among feminists about the wisdom of invoking maternity as a collective identity. In 1908, as her feminist compatriots claimed rights based on their motherhood, Pelletier warned against this strategy: "Never will childbirth give women a title of social importance. Future societies may build temples to maternity but they will do so only to keep women locked up inside."[30] More recently, feminists have worried about whether and how a validation of maternity might endorse essentialist visions of womanhood. In this connection there has been no shortage of writing by feminist philosophers and historians wending their way between a recognition of, on the one hand, the strength of feminist arguments based on motherhood and, on the other, the danger such arguments pose for confirming social stereotypes that attribute gender discrimination to nature.[31] In most of this work (with the exception, as I will discuss in what follows, of some feminists' attempts to reformulate psychoanalysis) the figure of the mother is taken literally. I want to suggest that when she indeed becomes the basis for feminist mobilization (and this is not always the case in the history of this movement), she is better understood as a fantasy echo, as the key to a scenario in which women merge into a vast, undifferentiated collective, the many becoming one through the power of maternal love.

The paradigmatic scenario is contained in an account by the English suffragist Emmeline Pethick Lawrence of the International Women's Conference held at The Hague to oppose war in 1915. There was, she said, "similarity in personality and dress of the delegates who occupied the body of the hall. There was nothing in general appearance to distinguish one nationality from another, and looking into our own hearts we beheld as in a mirror the hearts of all those who were assembled with us, because deep in our own hearts lies the common heart of humanity. We realised that the fear and mistrust that had been fostered between the peoples of the nations was an illusion. We discovered that at the bottom, peace was nothing more or less than communal love."[32] Though this writing can surely be explained simply as good feminist rhetoric in the context of massive imperialist warfare on an unheard-of scale, such an explanation misses the emotional force of the appeal. The description condenses the process by which women recognize their commonality; they are already similar in personality and appearance, but they are also involved in a process of identification that melds them into one. By beholding themselves and one another "as in a mirror," they realize that "fear and mistrust" (difference) is "an illusion," and they "discover" that peace is "communal love." What the women share is "the common heart of humanity," a metonymic displacement of the womb. The communal love that emanates from this heart is the all-encompassing, selfless, seemingly sexless love of mothers for their children. In the scene, everyone loves like a mother and is loved as a daughter—the reciprocity of love and desire is assumed. The dissolving of the boundaries between mothers and daughters constitutes the reclaiming of a certain "lost territory," the pre-Oedipal love of the mother, and it provides what Luce Irigaray and Julia Kristeva refer to as a nonphallic (and, in the context of patriarchal symbolism, subversive) jouissance.

Irigaray and Kristeva have suggested (following Lacan on this point) that it is the "murder" not of the father but of the mother (the obliteration of her body and the relegation to nature of her undeniably social role of reproduction) that is the founding act of Western civilization. The maternal fantasy offered by Pethick Lawrence restores the social role of mothers, for they are responsible for life, while men wage war and cause death. The love that emanates from these mothers, the positive community it generates, is only one side of the dual perception (good and bad, loving and hateful, life and death) of mothers that Melanie Klein theorizes,[33] and it is radically different from, and in tension with, the misogynist fantasy that psychoanalysts tell us associates loss of identity and even death with a mother's engulfing love.[34] Fantasies that provide the terms of political identification are undoubtedly selective; the one I have been describing sets itself against the other options (bad mothers, the mortal danger of incorporation) in its appeal to community. In addition, the feminist maternal fantasy, unlike the fantasy of the female orator, works to reconcile contradiction (in the way that the pregnant mother's body signifies and contains difference) and seems to lack the punishing dimensions of "A Child Is Being Beaten," perhaps because it calls on pre-Oedipal associations between mothers and children.

Here it may be helpful to follow Irigaray's reasoning. Offering a feminist variation on Lacan's suggestion that woman was associated with "a *jouissance* beyond the phallus,"[35] Irigaray seeks to detach woman from her definition as a function of man. She posits instead a sharp distinction between the "world of the flesh" (the body of the mother) and the "universe of language" (the law of the father). "The problem is that, by denying the mother her generative power and by wanting to be the sole creator, the Father, according to our culture, superimposes upon the archaic world of the flesh a universe of language and symbols" that subsume women to men.[36] Irigaray looks for a way of establishing an autonomous realm for women by bringing to light the "*jouissance* beyond the phallus" that patriarchal law repressed. She particularly emphasizes the attractions of the mother-daughter relationship and the positive aspects of identity between these two:

> Given that the first body [we/they] have any dealings with is a woman's body, that the first love they share is mother love, it is important to remember that women always stand in an archaic and primal relationship with what is known as homosexuality. . . . When analytic theory says that the little girl must give up her love of and for her mother, her desire of and for her mother, so as to enter into the desire of/for the father, it subordinates woman to a normative heterosexuality, normal in our societies, but completely pathogenic and pathological. Neither little girl nor woman must give up love for their mother. Doing so uproots them from their identity, their subjectivity. (44)

Much of Irigaray's writing is prescriptive; the future conditional articulates what always seemed to me an original late-twentieth-century utopian vision: "But if mothers could be made women, there would be a whole mode of a relationship of desiring speech between daughter and mother, son and mother, and it would, I think, completely rework the language [*langue*] that is now spoken" (52). In fact, I think there are historical precedents for Irigaray's formulations, evidence that corroborates her theoretical insights into the maternal fantasies that have at certain historical moments consolidated women under the banner of feminism. These fantasies don't evoke the maternal body and its flesh directly, if at all; rather, they refer to the ineffable quality of love. This love both avows and denies an explicitly sexual longing of and for the mother. As if in deference to patriarchal rules, it covers over its own transgression.

The invocation of the feminist maternal fantasy is evident in the 1840s and 1850s. In France, romantic Christianity blended with Saint-Simonian socialism to inspire Flora Tristan and Deroin in their rapturous visions of messianic maternal salvation. Tristan called on women, whose moral likeness, rooted in motherhood, erased differences of class, education, and wealth, to take the lead in establishing the "universal union of working men and women."

> Women, whose souls, hearts, spirits, senses are endowed with such sensitivity that . . . you have a tear for every sorrow,—a cry for every groan of anguish,—a sublime enthusiasm for every generous action,—a self-sacrifice for every suffering,—a consoling word for every affliction:—women, who are consumed by the need to love, to act, to live; who seek everywhere for an outlet for this burning and ceaseless activity of the soul which inspires you and consumes you, torments you, kills you; women,—will you remain silent and hidden forever, while the largest and most useful class, your brothers and sisters the proletarians, those who work, suffer, weep and groan, come and implore you to help them overcome misery and ignorance?[37]

The passion described is attributed to the soul, but the erotic quality of this "burning and ceaseless activity . . . which inspires . . . consumes . . . torments . . . kills" is undeniable. Tristan urged the male workers in her union to submit to women's leadership. "I pointed out," she reported, "that we had reached the reign of women,—that the reign of war, of brute force, had been that of [men] and that now women could achieve more than men because they had more love, and today love alone must rule."[38] Here was the theme of "communal love" and the end of all difference that would sound again in new form in 1915. In a similar voice, and in Tristan's wake, Deroin predicted a future characterized by harmony. Everyone would live peacefully in a large, social family, united by pure, maternal love: "The time of the reign of woman is near and humanity will quit the fatal path of progress through pain, of progress through struggle and poverty, to follow the providential path of peaceful and harmonious progress, led by the mother of humanity, Woman regenerated by liberty."[39] For Deroin and many of her associates, the jouissance of the fantasy came precisely from the juxtaposition of sex and purity, and the use of romantic, even erotic, language to characterize chaste and selfless maternal love. The mother, like the saintly mother of Christ, "acts because she loves. Love of humanity is eternal love."[40]

A later, more secular example of this feminist maternal fantasy comes from the call of the African American Mary Church Terrell in 1899 to white women to come to the aid of their black sisters, whose circumstances denied them the same thrill of joy at the contemplation of their children. "So rough does the way of her infant appear to many a poor black mother that instead of thrilling with the joy which you feel, as you clasp your little one to your breast, she trembles with apprehension and despair."[41] Overwhelming pride in one's children and the sensual pleasure of holding them ("thrill" and "joy" are signifiers of jouissance) are the feelings women are presumed to identify with across the vast differences of race and class. Mother and child, different and the same, women black and white, are to recognize one another through maternal love and then join in loving union—all differences effaced. The full account of the scene I referred to earlier— Verone's 1914 appeal to "all women of all nations, who suffer childbirth with the same pain"—illustrates the concrete unifying power of this vision. When Verone spoke, we are told, "a formidable cry of approval came from the audience, and it redoubled when a German delegate threw herself into the arms of Verone, and kissed her on both cheeks."[42] The reconciling force of maternal love brings a sisterly embrace; the scene is suffused with love, the healing, binding love of and for the mother. Through it, the women on the stage and in the audience become one. Echoing forward, we find Robin Morgan searching for the common ground of *Sisterhood Is Global.* Despite geographic, ethnic, religious, social, racial, and other diversities, she asks, "do we not, after all, easily recognize one another?"

> The underlying similarities emerge once we begin to ask sincere questions about differences. The real harem tradition included intense female friendship, solidarity, and high culture. . . . The real "belly dance" is a childbirth ritual celebrating life; the Rags al Sharqi . . . is meant as an exercise in preparation for labor and childbirth. . . . The examples could go on and on. . . . Is it any wonder that such words as daring, rebellion, journey, risk, and vision recur throughout *Sisterhood is Global* like refrains

punctuating the same basic story: one of deep suffering but also of a love—for life, children, men, other women, the land of one's birth, humanity itself—a love fierce enough to cleanse the world?[43]

"A love fierce enough to cleanse the world": though the terms and practices of motherhood varied profoundly from mid-nineteenth-century France to late twentieth-century America, they were subsumed—literally, in the fantasy scenario—by this idealization of love. What I have been calling a feminist maternal fantasy allowed the return of (what Irigaray and Kristeva differently think of as) a repressed jouissance. Its rearticulation served to consolidate feminist solidarity in the moment when it was invoked, in history and as history. Maternal love referred to a desire (her own, her children's) distinct from and potentially prior to that which is associated with heterosexuality, with phallic economies, with men. The world of women conjured by feminists in this fantasy is one in which women find pleasure among themselves, or "*jouissent d'elles-mêmes*" in Irigaray's words.[44] The historian's pleasure, it might be added, is in finding herself a party to this scene of feminine jouissance.

Conclusion

I am not seeking to discredit feminism by pointing to the importance of fantasy in enabling identifications that transcend history and national specificity. Instead, I want to argue that thinking about the operations of fantasy deepens our understanding of how a movement like feminism works and, at the same time, avoids attributing essentialist qualities to it. I am also not suggesting that these women were not really affected by discrimination, which disenfranchised them and denied them public access. The anxiety in the repeated scenes of female public oration, of course, comments on relations of power in the "real" world. My points are that power is produced in concrete and particular relationships, that subjects are structured as a function of those relationships, and that these subjects cannot transcend the specificity of their circumstances without the simplification fantasy provides. Similarly, I do not mean to argue that mothers lack real concern for their children's lives, though I do not think they have a natural (or indeed even an experientially based) antipathy to conflict and war. Instead, concepts of motherhood, and the very experience of being a mother, have varied by class and culture and historical epoch and have done so in many more ways than I have been able to discuss in this short essay. The fantasy of maternal love has provided feminists with a way of establishing a commonality based on unconscious associations, despite their differences, and this has been its efficacy

If, as analysts of identity, we think of these fantasy scenarios also as echoes and thus look for the distortions and diffractions—the individual variations of detail and figuration in them—we will be able to take into account the profound differences in the very being of women that it is the function of fantasy to efface. In that way we will deepen our appreciation of how some political movements use history to solidify identity and thereby build constituencies across the boundaries of difference that separate physical females from one another within cultures, between cultures, and across time.

I have restricted my attention in this essay to feminism, whose history is most familiar to me. But I think fantasy echo has much wider applicability, and not only to movements built on collective identities. The term usefully describes the figure of the "white sheik" detailed in the work of the anthropologist Steven Caton. The white sheik was a figure used by successive generations of European and American men to elaborate their relationships (variously as adventurers, entrepreneurs, spies, and clandestine military operatives) to the East by identifying with T. E. Lawrence as depicted (phantasmatically) in the film *Lawrence of Arabia*. These men resonate especially with the scene in which Lawrence dances, clothed in the flowing robes of a sheik (that endow him, if not with outright femininity, then with an ambiguous alternative to Western masculinity). Here, in the staging of his jouissance, Lawrence presents the lure of the Orient. The recurring fantasy scenario, as Caton has described it, was adjusted and adapted—in the mode of an echo—to different historical moments in the changing geopolitical ties between East and West.[45]

Fantasy echo is not a label that, once applied, explains identity. It is rather the designation of a set of psychic operations by which certain categories of identity are made to elide historical differences and create apparent continuities. Fantasy echo is a tool for analysts of political and social movements as they read historical materials in their specificity and particularity. It does not presume to know the substance of identity, the resonance of its appeal, or the transformations it has undergone. It presumes only that where there is evidence of what seems enduring and unchanging identity, there is a history that needs to be explored.

3. Feminist Reverberations

IN MARCH 1942, only a few months after the United States had entered the Second World War, the chairman of the program committee for the American Historical Association's annual meeting, the Yale historian Stanley Pargellis, wrote to the Hunter College professor Dorothy Ganfield Fowler in her capacity as secretary of the Berkshire Conference of Women Historians. He was turning to Mrs. Fowler (as he addressed her—he referred to all the men mentioned in the letter as "Professor") for some advice. The general theme for the 1942 meeting was, fittingly enough, "Civilization in Crisis," and the program committee (which initially had managed not to include a single woman in its ranks) hoped to organize a session on women and the great crises of civilization. Pargellis thought that if the right scholars (men or women) could be found, "we might produce an original and significant session of two or three papers, one on the changing functions of women in the fifth or the sixteenth centuries, and one on the nature of the problem today."[1] Fowler replied with the names of two scholars: Pearl Kibre, a medievalist, and Mary Sumner Benson, an Americanist working on the eighteenth and nineteenth centuries. And, showing herself to be a model of disciplinary rectitude, she suggested that the question of women's status in the present might best be addressed more informally by members of the audience, since little reliable material was available for serious research.[2] The following day, Pargellis brusquely turned down her proposal:

> Dear Mrs. Fowler, I am glad that you were interested in the subject about which I wrote you, but must confess that I was disappointed to find that so little attention has been given to the problem of the way in which the status of women reflects the character of a civilization. I gather from your letter that both Dr. Kibre and Dr. Benson have been concerned with descriptive treatments only, and that there is no one who could handle for the great critical periods a more interpretive approach. If my understanding of your letter is the right one, I think that we had better abandon plans for a session upon this important topic.[3]

Several days later, Fowler wrote back, assuring Pargellis that the scholars she had recommended were quite capable of interpretive approaches and offering to have the Berkshire Conference take over full responsibility for the session.[4] He replied that "without committing ourselves in any way," the program committee was willing to let the women historians explore some further possibilities. His letter went on to outline his expectations in a most condescending manner, defining terms ("by sweeping change we mean something more profound and more long range than a war") and time periods ("As for the American Revolution, we have come to the conclusion that it is of insufficient significance to stand along with the shift from medievalism to modernity as a period of crisis").[5] Fowler replied politely that she would take all this up with her colleagues at the forthcoming meeting of the Berkshire Conference, but there is no correspondence after that.[6] In any case, there was no annual meeting of the American Historical Association in December 1942. It was canceled at the request of the Office of Defense Transportation (the Department of Homeland Security of its day). Instead, the association published a series of papers that had been prepared for the meeting; not surprisingly, given this exchange of letters, the topic of women in history was not included.[7]

I cite this incident for several reasons. First, it allows us a moment of self-congratulation for the role of the Berkshire Conference in making women and women's history integral to the profession and the discipline. We've come a long way since the 1940s, at least as far as some feminist goals are concerned. And I think recognizing that fact and acknowledging the role of these early pioneers is a good way to begin this conference. Second (and this is not a reason for celebration), we are once again in a period of grave crisis, on the brink, it sometimes seems, of another world war. A generation of women's history writing—much of it nurtured by the Berkshire Conference, a crucible for theoretical and substantive debates of feminism—has guaranteed that this time we are in a position to provide critical interpretation. Feminism has taught us to analyze the operations of difference and the workings of power, and we can extend these analyses to many different arenas. What Wendy Brown has called a feminist analytics of power[8] is one of the lasting results of the second wave of feminist scholarship. Indeed, one of our early claims—that attention to women and gender would yield analyses of politics beyond the relationships of women and men—has been borne out repeatedly. The feminist analytics of power is my subject here. I want to reflect on its insights as they apply to the current crisis, to the history of women and gender, and to the themes of global and local that traverse these seemingly disparate fields.

"Fictitious Unities"

Although the title of the conference where I presented an earlier version of these reflections—"Local Knowledge ↔ Global Knowledge"—was chosen long before September 11, 2001, it poses a good problematic for a time of crisis, even though it carries none of the sense of urgency, anger, and despair that many of us have been feeling since the attacks. The arrows between the two spheres (local and global) point in both directions, implying interaction and exchange: two-directional flows of information, people, technology, markets, capital, natural resources, cultural objects, cultural meanings, and diseases and their cures. There's room in our analyses of the global and the local, if not in these iconic representations, for asymmetries of power, for domination and resistance, even for interpenetration and hybridity. What can't be captured by the title and those benign arrows (they are, after all, directional signals, not instruments of aggression) are the horrific images of terrorist attacks and relentless warfare that we have witnessed. The Twin Towers imploding, suicide bombs exploding, our weapons of mass destruction seeking to locate and destroy terrorists and their weapons of mass destruction, tanks crushing homes with residents still inside, a brutal occupying force wantonly destroying the infrastructure of an aspiring state. The wrenching scenes in newspapers and on television: faces contorted in unspeakable grief; refugees running and screaming, or silently fleeing smoke and fire; shattered families mourning their losses; bewildered civilians roaming through ruins, bloodied, homeless, and hungry; furious orators railing venomously against outside enemies; flags burning and insignias of hatred scrawled on ruined buildings; bitter accusations and gunshots exchanged across mined borders—Pakistan, India, Afghanistan, Israel, Lebanon, New York.[9] The threat of nuclear weapons is no longer containable by mutual assured destruction pacts of the Cold War era, so fears of devastation, once quieted, have returned. We ponder uneasily the connections between blood and oil: does the spilling of one guarantee the flow of the other? The leaders of America—now the only superpower—flagrantly violate the rules of law, domestic and international, that they claim it is their mission to protect. The USA Patriot Act, signed into law on October 26, 2001, eliminates judicial overview of the government in its surveillance of individuals and organizations and its restrictions of their activities; it authorizes searches, seizures, and detentions that might otherwise be unconstitutional. We have seen the internment of ethnically marked suspects on the flimsiest of grounds; the creation of military tribunals; the silencing of critical dissent (including the suspension in some universities of professors—usually themselves Arab but, in one case, a translator for an imprisoned Muslim cleric—for expressions of pro-Palestinian opinions); the unilateral abrogation of international treaties; flagrant disregard for such instruments of international law as the Geneva Conventions; and the reckless adoption of cowboy-style, "go it alone" diplomacy. All this has been justified in the name of an apocalyptic moral vision, revealed to these born-again cold warriors, whose actions seem to be intensifying rather than lessening the possibilities of greater and more dangerous conflicts. Clifford

Geertz's apt characterization, "The World in Pieces"—a metaphoric reference to the fracturing of identities and allegiances at local and global levels—now has the force of a literal prediction.[10] "Peace in the world," went our protest song of the 1950s, "or the world in pieces."

Stanley Pargellis's 1942 report to the American Historical Association was titled *The Quest for Political Unity in World History*. Today such a quest seems naive at best. And no one is offering world unity as a way out of the current crisis. Or, if they are, it is in stark, binary terms: alliances of good against axes of evil, Western secular rationalism against Islamic religious fundamentalism, modernity against primitive tribalism, reason of state against the forces of terrorism. Lines are being drawn and categories produced to give schematic coherence to the messy entanglements of local, national, regional, and international politics.

As feminists we have learned to be wary of such categories—Denise Riley has dubbed them "fictitious unities"—because even as they offer terms for identification, they create hierarchies and obscure differences that need to be seen.[11] (Paradoxically, the fact that they are fictitious makes their effects no less real.) "Men" and "women," we now know, are not simple descriptions of biological persons, but representations that secure their meanings through interdependent dichotomies: strong/weak, active/passive, reasonable/emotional, public/private, political/domestic, mind/body. One term gains its meaning in relation to the other and also to other binary pairs nearby. Indeed, the Other is a crucial (negative) factor for any positive identity—and the positive identity stands in superior relation to the negative. Women's supposed lack of reason has historically not only been a justification for denying them education or citizenship, it has also served to depict reason as a function of masculinity. The boundaries of public and private have not reflected the existing roles of men and women but have instead created them, with the imagined map of gender territories becoming the referent not only for social organization, but for the very meanings (social, cultural, and psychological) of the differences between the sexes. If the meanings of difference are created by contrasting categories, within the categories coherent identities are produced by denying differences. So although the term "women" historically has served to consolidate feminist movements, it has also made race, class, ethnicity, religion, sexuality, and nationality somehow secondary, as if these distinctions among us (and the hierarchical positioning that accompanies them) mattered less than the physical similarities we share. At least since the 1980s, feminist scholarship has learned (often quite painfully—think of the bitter challenges posed by women of color to the hegemony of white women, by lesbians to mainstream feminism's normative heterosexuality, and by Eastern European women to the presumed superiority of Western feminist theory) to make nuanced distinctions along multiple axes of difference; its theories no longer assume fixed relationships between entities but treat them as the mutable effects of temporally, culturally, and historically specific power dynamics. The mantra of "race, class, gender" was a way of thematizing—and so rigidifying and therefore reducing the applicability of—what is in fact a much more open analytic approach. The premises of this approach are what is important, and they are what inform necessarily detailed readings of specific situations. If there is something that can be called feminist methodology, it might be summarized by these axiomatic statements: there is neither a self nor a collective identity without an Other; there is no inclusiveness without exclusion, no universal without a rejected particular, no neutrality that doesn't privilege an interested point of view; and power is always an issue in the articulation of these relationships. Put in other words, we might say that all categories do some kind of productive work; the questions are how, and to what effect.

We need this feminist methodology in the current crisis. It should make us pause at the binary divisions of the world into good and evil; at the phantasmatic evocation of a centuries-old crusade to the death by Islam against the West—even when it is offered by reputable scholars such as Samuel Huntington and Bernard Lewis.[12] How like those misogynistic fantasies of sexually frenzied women turning the world upside down these predictions are: reason threatened by passion, order by disorder, liberal tolerance consumed by rampant fanaticism, enlightenment endangered by the dark forces of sex and superstition—primal conflicts (figured as castration or incorporation) depicted as timeless and as foretelling the end of time. Certainly this way of thinking *is* the end of history and of politics.

Look at the Israeli-Palestinian conflict, depicted as the encounter between two opposing and equal forces: Jews and (Palestinian) terror-ists. Taking advantage of September 11, Ariel Sharon and others have written this very particular Middle Eastern conflict into the larger Manichaean script. Official Israeli and American rhetoric takes no account of significant details or of the political dynamics of an unequal relationship: the effects of Israeli occupation (which can only be called a form of state terrorism), of the steady expansion of Jewish settle-ments in defiance of Oslo and other accords, of the humiliations and deprivations visited daily, over the years, on Palestinians within Israel and in the West Bank and Gaza. Instead, Israel is depicted as an unwarranted victim of Palestinian rage, drawing on an association of Jews with the Holocaust, which is not appropriate in this situation. Yes, there are terrible and inexcusable attacks on Israeli civilians, but the state of Israel is not a victim; it is a mighty nuclear power, an occupying force. Without excusing or condoning suicide bombings, we can read them as weapons of the weak; symptoms of terrible injustices, which include the denial to the Palestinians of the kind of institutional foun-dations that would enable them to engage in alternative (and more peaceful) forms of politics or even more acceptable forms of warfare. Is it any wonder that those treated brutally reply in kind? That those left outside the law (Palestinians are not equal citizens within Israel, nor do they have a state of their own) behave illegally?[13] There are undeniable differences between English suffragists and suicide bomb-ers, and I don't mean to equate them in any way, but wasn't the message of the English suffragists who set fires and broke windows in the early 1900s that we shouldn't expect lawful behavior from those who are not allowed to make laws? And isn't the idea that violent feminist actions are proof of women's hysterical nature analogous to the treatment of any protest by Palestinians as inherently terroristic—as if terrorism were an essential trait of Palestinians?

The good-versus-evil opposition doesn't only wipe out the particu-lar conditions of this conflict and mask the vast inequalities between the sides. It also makes the differences within each side—for the contestations of politics—hard to see or hear. If you're critical of Israel's policies, you're anti-Semitic; if you think there's a case to be made for Palestine, you're an apologist for terror. In a perverse way, this reductive categorizing has opened up new space for expressions of traditional anti-Semitism—Jews as a group have become a target not only for those opposed to Israel's actions, but also for racists who have long hated Jews. And it has deprived of a voice those critics of Israel who are not anti-Semitic. There have, of course, been attempts to challenge these categorizations: many Europeans and their leaders have rejected the simplistic oppositions, calling for a more historicized understanding of the conflict (though they have been bitterly denounced as anti-Semites by Benjamin Netanyahu and Ariel Sharon); and there are a number of petitions signed by Jews who deliberately invoke their group identity to dissociate themselves from Israel's policies. Still the overwhelming pressure, here at least, is to deploy essentialist categories, to homogenize identity, to make difference a matter of moral qualities rather than of politics and history. As feminists we know that the ruses of essentialism—whatever guises they adopt—ultimately perpetuate inequalities and militate against change. Women need not be the explicit object of debate for us to deploy our analytics of power to useful effect.

But when women are the object of campaigns by the forces of good against the forces of evil, it is important that we use our methodologies to read what's going on. The cynical attempt to make the wars in Afghanistan and Iraq into crusades on behalf of women's emancipation ought not to confuse feminists, and not only because concern for the rights of women was not exactly a priority of the Bush administration before September 11. Rather, what informs our skepticism is our understanding of the ways that oppositional categories work to eliminate contradiction and create the illusion of homogeneity (all of us on the good side must believe the same things). The conflation of terrorism and women's oppression erases any problems the good side may face (where there is no terrorism, it follows that there is no oppression of women), and it rallies the support of some potential internal critics (such as feminists, liberals, and human rights advocates). "The fight against terrorism is also a fight for the rights and dignity of women," first lady Laura Bush told the nation in a radio address in November 2001. "The brutal oppression of women," she said, "is the central goal of the terrorists." Not all Muslims are terrorists, she added (making a distinction not always observed by the FBI and other parts of the Department of Justice): "Only the terrorists and the Taliban forbid education to women. Only the terrorists and the Taliban threaten to pull out women's fingernails for wearing nail polish."[14] (All bases are covered here: equality feminists get education, difference feminists get nail polish!) For good measure, Defense Secretary Donald Rumsfeld joined the chorus, attributing Afghan women's newfound freedoms to our "recent military victories against the Taliban." Not only had restrictive dress codes been lifted, he crowed, but the beating of women for the "crime of laughing in public" had ended.[15] (I find it hard to imagine Afghan women laughing—in public or private—as American bombs rained down on their villages. And I wonder, too, about what fixing on women's laughter in public as a sign of their freedom tells us about Rumsfeld's imagination and about his conception of rights.) I don't mean to imply here that the Taliban treated women well, just that these simplistic equations of good and evil, virtue and terror, us and them don't offer credible diagnoses of, or solutions for, the problems of Afghan (or for that matter any) women. In addition, they promote a particular vision of women as victims, specifically of "other" women (Third World, Middle Eastern, or Islamic) as in need of saving by the West. If we follow our own theoretical insights, this inevitably creates a hierarchy that promotes and reinforces a sense not just of Western superiority, but of Western women's superiority—the old colonial relationship emerges intact in an operation of domination disguised as a mission of salvation. Lila Abu-Lughod warns against the very strong appeal of such rescue campaigns. "When you save someone," she reminds us, "you are saving them from something. You are also saving them to something. What violences are entailed in this transformation? And what presumptions are being made about the superiority of what you are saving them to? This is the arrogance that feminists need to question."[16]

Using the salvation of women to justify the war in Afghanistan had a broader resonance; it not only reconfigured a complex geopolitical engagement (in which oil pipelines, among other material issues, play no small part) into a simple battle against terrorism, it also used recognizable gender references to articulate power relations between protector and protected. As feminists we are rightly skeptical of turning our fate over to those who promise protection, who justify their actions (whether aggressive, repressive, or merely taken without consulting us) in the name of our security. (Indeed, one of the criticisms of the Taliban was that they justified their treatment of women as "protection.") As Iris Marion Young has argued, the central logic of this kind of protection is masculinist, and it assumes "the subordinate relation of those in the protected position. In return for male protection, the woman concedes critical distance and decision making autonomy."[17] Extending the analysis, Young argues that however benign it seems, state-sponsored protection denies citizens the role they ought to play in democratic societies:

> Through the logic of protection the state demotes members of a democracy to dependents. State officials adopt the stance of masculine protector, telling us to entrust our lives to them, not to question their decisions about what will keep us safe. Their protector position puts us, the citizens and residents who depend on their strength and vigilance for our security, in the position of women and children under the charge of the male protector. Because they take the risks and organize the agency of the state, it is their prerogative to determine the objectives of protective action and their means. In a security regime there is no room for separate and shared powers, nor for questioning and criticizing the protector's decisions and orders. Good citizenship in a security regime consists in cooperative obedience for the sake of the safety of all.[18]

The relations established by the logic of protection are multiple and complex: the protector is the United States and so American women, too, are positioned as protectors of the rest of the world; but domestically, women along with most of the population are in the feminine position of dependency and subordination to the government. The administration's point of view becomes the only true one, even if the facts have to be fabricated by a special arm of the Department of Defense (an activity proposed in the early days of the war in Afghanistan). One of the premises of feminism over the years has been that equality for women means better and more democracy. "Democracy without women is not democracy," was the slogan of feminists in the European Union in the 1980s and 1990s. The validity of this claim seems borne out by Young's analysis of the security regime and its logic of protection. Dependency and subordination are never in the best interests of the protected, for they rule out real participation, denying agency and silencing those voices that might have something different to propose.

Reverberations

We need the feminist analysis of categories of identity not only to detect the differentials of power constructed by binary oppositions that are purported to be timeless, natural, and universal, but also to contextualize and historicize these categories. Feminist methodology has taught us to ask about variation, difference, and conflict whenever we are presented with neatly contained entities—and not only "man" and "woman." We ought to assume, relying on our methodology even if we lack expertise in the particular field, that there is neither a uniform Islam, nor a single entity called the Middle East. These are politically convenient labels that mask the varieties of states and regimes in the region, as well as of religious movements, including Islamic feminisms that offer new interpretations of the Koran to legitimize claims for changes in women's status. It is these feminisms, strange to our traditions of secular individualism, that Fatima Gailani (a member of the Grand Council that deliberated the political reconstruction of Afghanistan) reminds us, that need a certain recognition and autonomy. She urged American feminists to press for a US foreign policy that would not "save" Afghan women to our values but would create the kinds of conditions that would permit them to participate fully in necessarily heated debates about the future of their own country.[19]

We have learned—sometimes with great difficulty—to acknowledge these very different feminisms, to accept the fact that feminism refers to a multiplicity of often conflicting movements. Speaking of the global and the local, even using two-directional arrows, doesn't quite capture it. There may be a recognizable core of meaning, but feminism (like any such concept) needs to be understood as if in translation. Anna Tsing has told us that these are always "faithless translations," since linguistic and cultural differences as well as specific uses affect the meanings of terms.[20] Echo may be a better metaphor than translation for designating the mutability of words or concepts because it is more mobile, connoting not just a distorted repetition but also movement in space and time—history.[21] Perhaps in these days of cataclysmic transmission, it would be better still to talk about reverberations, seismic shock waves moving out from dispersed epicenters, leaving shifted geological formations in their wake. The word "reverberation" carries a sense both of causes of infinite regression—reverberations are subsequent echoes, successions of echoes—and of effect—reverberations are also repercussions.

Reverberation occurs to me, I think, because it's the best way to characterize circuits of influence these days. It applies well to the case of France, where in June 2000 feminists succeeded in passing a law on parity that requires equal numbers of women and men to be candidates for most elections. The events of September 11 and the Middle East conflict have been a setback for implementation of the parity law, however. In the 2002 French presidential elections, the right-wing nationalist Jean-Marie Le Pen made a strong enough showing to secure a place in the second round of the contest. Le Pen's appeal was anti-immigrant, which in France means anti-Muslim. Martial Bourquin, the Socialist mayor of Audincort, one of the towns that voted heavily for Le Pen's National Front, explained that hostility to Muslim immigrants, who constituted some 15 percent to 20 percent of the local population, had intensified before the elections. "What happened in New York, Afghanistan, in the Middle East has deepened the religious divide" here, he said.[22] (France is surely not the only place in which local tensions have been recast in terms of "insecurity" in the face of threats of terrorism [which now includes everything from juvenile crime to movements of resistance within authoritarian states] and whose electoral results [a strong showing of the far Right] have had repercussions at home and on the international scene.) In an effort to stave off legislative victories by Le Pen's party, the centrist and left parties in France decided not to implement parity in their selection of candidates for the elections to the National Assembly in 2002. Since "it's a matter of winning," one party leader commented, the risk of running women is too great. If a temporary setback for French feminists is one of the repercussions of September 11, there are other reverberations of the parity movement itself that have been more positive. Taking up the argument that citizenship means not just voting but holding office, women from Mexico to the United

Kingdom, and from India to the United States, have been pressing for laws to increase their numbers as representatives. This is an example of an idea catching on, being adapted as it moves, working differently in different contexts.

Reverberation is a good way to think about this global circulation of feminist strategies, of feminism itself, and also of the analytic term "gender." Both "gender" and "feminism" are usually taken to have Anglo-American origins; indeed, for some critics they are an example of the one-way trajectory of globalization, in the transmission of goods or ideas. Thus feminism has been reviled as one of those commodities "made in the USA" that corrupts the culture of traditional societies, and gender (of similar provenance) has been taken to constitute a threat to the natural or "God-given" distinctions between the sexes. In fact, neither feminism nor gender are homogeneous even at their points of origin (if we can even identify such points): the forms they take and the meanings given to them are adapted to local circumstances, which then have international reverberations of their own. What ultimately unites them, as I have argued in chapter 2, is a phantasmatic identification across temporal and spatial lines of difference.

Take the example of "gender," a term that emanated from American feminist circles. Even here, though, there was no fixed meaning beyond the idea of "social sex." Since "sex" connotes both biology and sexual relations (sexuality), it immediately complicates "gender." There were feminists who took sexual difference as a given, the ground on which gender systems were then built; there were others who took sexual difference to be the effect of historically variable discursive practices of "gender." The first approach made much of the sex/gender distinction and focused on cultural construction—the assignment of roles and the attribution of traits to sexed individuals—deliberately leaving aside the question of nature. The research these feminists undertook tended to be empirical: histories of exemplary women; recoveries of women writers and artists; statistical demonstrations of occupational and wage discrimination; and documentation of the sexism of doctors, priests, educators, and politicians. The second approach rejected the sex/gender, nature/culture dichotomy. "If the immutable character of sex is contested," writes Judith Butler, "perhaps this construct called 'sex' is as culturally constructed as gender; indeed, perhaps it was always already gender, with the consequence that the distinction between sex and gender turns out to be no distinction at all."[23] Research undertaken from this vantage point asked how knowledge of sex and sexual difference was produced and institutionalized, and it was often informed by poststructuralist and psychoanalytic theory.

But the clarity of our empiricist / theoretical divide blurred as feminists around the world took up the term "gender," sometimes translating it (often with great difficulty), sometimes leaving it untranslated. Either way, there were revealing tensions, terrifically interesting subversions that might, for example, turn sex into gender or gender into sex.[24] In Eastern Europe different theoretical uses of "gender" had everything to do with particular political positions. Those looking for ways to counter rightist conservative notions of the natural or God-given facts of biology appropriated theories that deconstructed binary oppositions and emphasized the indeterminacy and variety, as well as the mutability, of differences attributed to biological sex. In contrast, those contending with leftist conservatisms that took equality to mean the obliteration of difference (usually the subsuming of women into the category "Man") sought ways of making sexual difference, and the social inequalities it engenders, a central tenet of their theorizing and a visible fact of life. For them, statistical documentation was critical if social policy were to address gender inequalities. And it didn't matter that sexual difference (or nature) might be reified in the process, since the point was to demonstrate that sex was now, but should not in the future be, a ground for unequal social treatment. Depending on particular local conditions, feminists in different postcommunist countries faced different constellations of these conservatisms; depending on their own politics, they combined different theoretical insights to formulate their strategies. These new combinations then echoed across international boundaries, in the forums of the United Nations and elsewhere, to be picked up and readjusted in new circumstances for other strategic reasons.

We can tell similar stories about the reverberations of feminism. I want to tell two. The first is about Julia Kristeva, most often referred to as a French feminist (along with Hélène Cixous and Luce Irigaray). In the debates among US feminists in the 1980s, French feminism was equated with poststructuralist theories of language and psychoanalysis and with an emphasis on difference; it was counterposed to a more empirical, social-scientific Anglo-American feminism, which emphasized equality. This contrast, of course, obscured many things, among them the numbers of French scholars and activists committed to social science and equality, and the numbers of Anglo-Americans who embraced poststructuralism. More interesting, perhaps, it erased a history of cross-fertilization that confounds not only the French / American opposition, but the one that came into prominence in the 1990s between Eastern European and Western feminism. Julia Kristeva was born and educated in Bulgaria, where she began her career as an interpreter of Mikhail Bakhtin. Bakhtin developed his historicized version of structuralism (a variant of the structuralist semiotics of Iurii Lotman and the structuralism of Roman Jakobson, to name only a few of those working in this field at the time) as a way of challenging Stalinist dogma. Bakhtin's emphasis on formal textual readings was meant to replace the crude sociological characterizations of artistic and cultural productions used in official Soviet parlance; the suggestion that meanings were shaped dialogically contradicted the communist state's belief that language could be policed and signs controlled.[25] Kristeva moved to Paris in the mid-1960s, bringing Bakhtin's notion of polyphony to French structuralist debates, and she coined the term "intertextuality" to lend (in her words) "dynamism to structuralism."[26] What came to be called French feminism, then, was crucially influenced by philosophical movements opposing communism in Eastern Europe, and by a theory that posited not the clash of differences but interaction as the basis for communication.

This history undermines the presumed superiority to Eastern Europeans of those Western feminists in the 1990s who offered what they called (in the singular) "feminist theory" as the solution to the problems of women in the postcommunist era. The more complicated history of the 1970s is that while some English and American feminists were trying to reconcile Marxism and feminism (in the context of the New Left), Eastern European feminists in movements of resistance rejected the official theory of communist states by embracing versions of structuralism and then of poststructuralism. As Miglena Nikolchina has shown, there was plenty of theory in Eastern Europe before and after the fall of communism, and some strands of Western feminism

had already felt its reverberations.[27] But the sharp differentiation between East and West offered in the 1990s more often attributed theory
to the West, leaving the East to fill in the blanks with empirical data.
(Western foundations—Soros, Ford—exacerbated the problem by
paying for translations of Western feminist writings into Eastern European languages but not Eastern writings into Western languages.)
This East/West divide and its accompanying erasure of history—the
general intellectual history of the region and the particular histories,
both intellectual and political, of the many variants of communism in
Poland, Hungary, Yugoslavia, and so forth—had many repercussions.
They ran the spectrum from tensions in the East/West Feminist
Network to the far more disturbing actions of Catherine MacKinnon
on behalf of raped Croatian women. Lacking knowledge of the intri-
cacies of Yugoslav politics and of the beleaguered multicultural feminist networks operating there, MacKinnon ended up allied with Croatian nationalists, whose concern about raped women stopped at their
own borders and did not prevent them from supporting the rapes of
Bosnian or Serbian women as legitimate acts of war.[28] MacKinnon's
action had repercussions: although she surely drew attention to one
aspect of the outrages of ethnic cleansing, she lost the opportunity to
offer a critique of the virulent nationalism that fueled it, and she made
life more dangerous for those Yugoslav feminists who were trying to
offer that critique. These included feminists known as Women in
Black, who, beginning in 1991, took to the streets in silent protest.
Theirs is the second story about the reverberations of feminism that I
want to tell.

Women in Black (WIB) was started in Jerusalem in January 1988
(at the time of the first Intifada) by women protesting the Israeli
occupation of the West Bank and Gaza. Once a week at the same
hour and in the same location—a major traffic intersection—a group
of women dressed in black raised a sign in the shape of a hand that
bore the message: "Stop the Occupation."[29] The idea spread quickly
to other places in Israel, where Palestinian and Jewish women often
stood together, and then to other countries, where solidarity vigils
were held in support of the Israeli women's actions. "Around 1990,"
according to an old WIB web page no longer available, "Women in
Black vigils took on a life of their own." They were held in many

countries and often had nothing to do with the Israeli occupation. In Italy, WIB protested the violence of the Mafia; in Germany, they stood against neo-Nazi attacks on migrant workers. In India, they called for an end to religious fundamentalists' mistreatment of women. Since 1991 in the former Yugoslavia—in Belgrade, Zagreb, and other cities—WIB has protested the ethnic nationalism that engulfed the country in wartime and that continues to define politics there. In May 2000 in Fiji, WIB emerged to protest the overthrow of the country's democratically elected government. In 2001 there were at least 123 regular WIB demonstrations held all over the world, some in centers of conflict, others in solidarity with vigils elsewhere. Some of the vigils have endured for years—their members have even held international meetings—while others come and go as events seem to require them. Their impact varies, in part depending on their proximity to the violence they protest. Activism is harder and more dangerous for the Women in Black in Israel, Serbia, or Kosovo than it is for their supporters in London or New York (except, of course, when the foreign supporters turn up on site, as some did in Ramallah in 2001 or when—as in the aftermath of September 11 in San Francisco—the supporters become the object of an investigation by the FBI because of their pro-Palestinian "international connections").[30] The farther away from specific politics supporters get, the more difficult it is to aim at clear political targets—as WIB in London discovered when they assembled to protest the NATO bombings of Serbia and Kosovo.[31] The abstract goal of peace was easily overcome by other goals, they learned, and they called off their action when they found themselves standing next to pro-Milošević, pro-Serbian nationalist demonstrators. But it is clear that as an international movement, WIB has attained a certain recognition as a political force. In 2001 one woman from Belgrade and another from Kosovo accepted the UN Millennium Peace Prize for Women on behalf of the international network of WIB. And WIB was nominated for a Nobel Prize by members of the parliaments of Denmark and Norway.

It is hard to imagine awarding these prizes to a phenomenon that is not an actual organization. The amazing thing about WIB is that it is an improvisational strategy, deployed locally rather than as a branch of any centralized association. WIB is (in the words of the women themselves) "a world-wide network of women committed to peace with justice and actively opposed to injustice, war, militarism and other forms of violence," not in the abstract but in specific situations. To use their words again, they are "not an organisation, but a means of communicating and a formula for action."[32] The practical means of mobilization are lists of telephone numbers and e-mail addresses, chains of affiliation among individuals. This enables "a form of activism . . . unique among oppositional parties and groups. . . . The activities of Women in Black developed in various phases according to immediate political needs, a quick response to everyday political reality."[33] The symbolism is multifaceted: a concrete manifestation of the body politic (of those bodies that produce the citizenry of a nation) and their paradoxical agency in the face of oppressive power—paradoxical because the mute, nonviolent witness signifies powerlessness while it offers a message of peace as the only rational alternative to catastrophe. The action is the same (all women, all in black, standing silently and peacefully in a public place at a regularly scheduled day and time), but its aim varies depending on the political context that the women have chosen to address. They stand as feminists, and they make no claim to be natural-born peacemakers. Yet they invoke a certain commonality: "women dressed in black as in New York, the fashion center of the world, and at the same time as in more primitive times where women's duty was to dress and mourn in black."[34] They do argue that women "are often at the receiving end of gendered violence in both peace and war, and [that] women are the majority of refugees." But it is their feminist analysis, not their feminine nature, that leads them to see "masculine cultures as specially prone to violence" and that gives them "a particular perspective on security" and war.

WIB deploys what I have been calling the feminist analytics of power in concrete (and different) political contexts. The group's actions contradict official pronouncements about enemies and friends, refusing to accept—and thus make real—membership in the "fictitious unities" offered by their leaders. Instead they literally demonstrate the complex realities of politics that acknowledge interconnected histories. Thus in Israel, WIB unites Palestinian and Jewish women in defiance of the idea that they belong to necessarily antagonistic sides. In Belgrade, WIB embraced multiethnic alliances, reminding their fellow citizens of the fact that Serbs, Croats, and Bosnians had for several generations lived side by side, intermarried, and shared citizenship until nationalist aggression drove them apart. In August 2001, the Serbian WIB called for an end to armed violence among Albanians, Turks, Serbs, and Macedonians in Macedonia. At the time of the NATO bombings in 1998, they were attacked as "Serbia's inner enemies," "quislings" in the service of the United States, and their demonstrations were banned. Their annual report that year was a "confession of guilt" for seven years of activism in opposition to ethnic homogenization and militarism. The report was based on or became the basis for (I'm not sure which) a poem, "Confession," written by Jasmina Tešanović[35] who explains how she had come to write it. On October 9, 1998, in Belgrade

> the last anniversary standing of Women in Black took place. . . . It had a grave ceremonial character, on the verge of civil war, of the renewed threat of NATO bombs. . . . The women dressed in black were standing in the ritual circle with long mottoes written on long flags whilst the new sympathizers and participants were talking among themselves. . . . I had a concrete feeling that an opposition existed in my town, in my country, and that Women in Black gave us form, public space and language. The conceptual action of this anniversary was a table with 100 papers on each of which was printed in big letters I CONFESS.[36]

Here is the poem that was based on these papers. It is a clear demonstration of applied feminist methodology that is at once familiar to us and distinctive; we hear it as an echo, we feel it as a reverberation.

I CONFESS:
I, Jelena, 12 years of age, confess only to life
J'accuse
That in 1991 I was against war, and I am now
I simply confess
That I will never be loyal to these authorities and
that I love Sabahet and Mira and Vjosa and Ana
To everything you wrote
That I am loyal to non-violence, solidarity, friendship and
that I am disloyal to all forms of authoritative power, violence, hate
That I can no longer stand it and that I can't take it anymore

That I have lived two lives, one in Sarajevo and one in Belgrade
That I did not wish for all that happened to us, but
I could not stop it
To all the charges, I confess that I am a traitor in every sense
That I am a traitor of the dominant militaristic values in Serbian
    society
That I will protest against all forms of violence, war and
    discrimination
That I sang Bosnian songs and danced Albanian dances throughout
    the whole war
That I hate war, violence and killing
I confess, but I also accuse
That violence in Kosovo cannot stop in the presence of the Serbian
    police.
But it can with international forces which will allow peace and
    process of negotiation
That there is no way I will go to the army.
Put militarism in the trash where it belongs
I confess that I will not give up my convictions, even if I wind up in
    prison
That from the beginning of the peace movement
I have been an active participant in all anti-war gatherings
That I will organize yet one more anti-war campaign
if you keep up this
bullshit
That I am European, a citizen of the world and that I am
an irreconcilable
opponent to this regime
That I respect the human rights of the Other and that first and
    foremost I consider myself
    a citizen
That I do not recognize war, discrimination, criminals and
    hopelessness
That for seven years I have plotted against this Nazi regime
That I am bitter about the fact that the authorities in Serbia and
    Yugoslavia constantly wage war
That conflicts should be resolved through negotiation and not
    violence
No passaran![37]

What is embodied here is not just dissent from the ruling power of the state (a refusal to sanction its actions ceremonially and in practice: "I will never be loyal"; "I am a traitor"), but active transgression of its boundaries ("I sang Bosnian songs and danced Albanian dances"; "I am European, a citizen of the world"; "I have lived two lives, one in Sarajevo and one in Belgrade"). These are agents of resistance (responsible citizens) who insist that there are, have been, and will be again democratic political alternatives to the regimes under which they have been forced to live.

What is striking about WIB, in contrast to many earlier feminist peace movements, is that it does not rely on a claim about the sameness of women or the unity of feminists. Instead, WIB's existence as "a means of mobilization and a formula for action" presumes fundamental differences among feminists: differences of context, history, and understandings of the feminine and of feminism itself. International gatherings, like the one held in Novi Sad to mark the tenth anniversary of the Serbian vigils, have drawn as many as 250 women from sixteen countries. These meetings provide a chance for the exchange of information and the identification of new targets, but there is no attempt to elaborate a common platform beyond an opposition to militarism and violence. The recognition of difference is fundamental, even as the form of protest and the name taken to describe the protesters is the same. According to the Women in Black website, "Each group is autonomous, each group focuses on the particular problems of personal and state violence in its part of the world." WIB embodies feminism as a situated strategic operation; it is not a question of global combined with local, but of echoes and reverberations that traverse the world. Without explicitly acknowledging the importance of imagined solidarities—fantasies that bridge differences, that find shared desire in different settings—these women enact scenarios that bring those solidarities into existence.[38]

The Traces of History

I take Women in Black to be an example of the feminist analytics of power in action, only one of the reverberations of the last decades of the theorizing and honing of our methodologies.[39] (I do not mean to endorse it as the best or most creative form feminist politics can take; I offer it only as a good example of feminist reverberations.) Here is a movement that is not narrowly restricted to things of interest to women, but that takes the domain of large-scale politics as its own. It punctures inflated dreams of national unity; exposes the toxicity of ethnic cleansing; and insists on the possibility of mutual recognition, rather than the dissolution of differences. It refuses to accept prevailing arrangements of power as natural or inevitable, insisting that better alternatives be considered. And, to recall the slogan of an earlier era, it "speaks truth to power"; the gesture of silent witness sharply rebukes those who would render us dependents by claiming to rule on our behalf.

But in this gesture—the standing still of women, all in black, silent and disapproving—there is also an undeniable echo of an earlier history: a feminist politics that rested on the moral infallibility of women who, as mothers, put the interests and care of others above their own. The appeal to "all women of all nations, who suffer childbirth with the same pain" launched the Women's International League for Peace and Freedom as the First World War began; it informed the many peace movements of the first and second waves of feminism; and it is still, for some, what makes global sisterhood possible.[40] Although WIB studiously avoids any call to action or claim to unity on the ground of maternalism, the echoes of this essentialism in these women-only demonstrations still seem audible. And they are testimony to the fact that reverberations are not only contemporaneous (running horizontally, circling the globe), but historical (running vertically, through time).[41] Feminism is constituted by its methods, theory, and history. We carry our pasts into the present, but never entirely. If we have extended the reach of our politics well beyond protests against gender discrimination, we have echoed, but not restated, an old feminist claim that women's interests were society's interests. There is repetition, but not seamless continuity because the repetition itself makes a difference, *is* a difference. Perhaps it is precisely an awareness of the inevitability and omnipresence of difference that distinguishes our understanding from that of our predecessors—difference as a fact of human existence, an instrument of power, an analytic tool, and a feature of feminism itself.

The difference, though, is not a sharp contrast but a succession of echoes, reverberations. The Berkshire Conference was one of those reverberations. It took its name and inspiration from a hardy band of women determined to foster collegiality and intellectual exchange among themselves and to improve their situation within the American Historical Association. Although we can identify with Dorothy Fowler's resistance to Stanley Pargellis, admire her persistence, and envy her patience (at least I do), our feminism is different from hers. We live in a different world: postcolonial, post–Cold War, postmodern. It's hard to find a way to detail the differences that separate the two periods without resorting to the binary thinking I've been criticizing. Only the distance of time and the myopia that accompanies it lets us describe Fowler's task as simpler than ours, our tools as sharper than hers. That's why reverberations are a better way of thinking about our relationship to feminist history. The reverberations of feminism have not usually been earth shattering, but they have created all kinds of disturbances, both laterally and longitudinally. We relish these disturbances because at their best they are intransigent and transgressive, paradoxical and subversive. And they always leave effects in their wake: sometimes visible, sometimes imperceptible, both conscious and unconscious, these are realignments and rearrangements that are social, political, and personal. They affect our very beings—as women, as citizens, and as situated strategic actors making a difference in our worlds.

4. Sexularism

On Secularism and Gender Equality

THE TITLE OF THIS CHAPTER began as a typographical error.[1] Each time I wrote secularism, I hit an *x* instead of a *c*. It happened so many times that I thought I should try to figure out what was going on. It is true that the two keys are adjacent on the keyboard, but they require different fingers in the touch-typing method I was taught years ago. So I wondered, thinking of Freud, if this wasn't a message from the unconscious, a slip of the finger if not of the tongue. The mistake, if it was one, did convey something of what I was thinking about this large and unwieldy topic: that in recent invocations of the secular, the issues of sex and sexuality get entangled in the wrong way.

The most frequent assumption is that secularism encourages the free expression of sexuality, and that it thereby ends the oppression of women because it removes transcendence as the foundation for social norms and treats people as autonomous individuals, pleasure-seeking agents capable of crafting their own destiny.[2] In substituting imperfect human initiative for the unquestioned truth of divine will, we are told, secularism broke the hold of traditionalism and ushered in the democratic modern age. The definitions of modernity are quite varied, but they typically include individualism, which in some accounts—feminists' among them—is equated with sexual liberation. History is remarkably absent from these accounts, except as teleology: the universal idea inevitably expands its applications and effects over time.

These days, secularism comes up frequently in discussions of Islam, which is said to hold on to values and ways of being that are at odds with modernity. In contemporary debates about Muslims—which focus on whether they can be integrated into Western societies, whether their culture is fundamentally at odds with "ours," and whether their values are compatible with political democracy—secularism is usually the unquestioned standard of judgment. It is taken to be an idea, either timeless or evolving, that signifies a universal project of human emancipation specifically including women. Whether the reference is to Iranian theocracy, the punitive behavior of the Taliban, or to immigrant populations in Europe, there is a particular emphasis on the plight of women in head scarves, veils, and burqas. For ideologues of French republicanism justifying a ban on Islamic head scarves in public schools, primordial values—or at least those inherited from the French Revolution—are what is at stake. The head of the commission recommending the ban on head scarves said: "France cannot allow Muslims to undermine its core values, which include a strict separation of religion and state, equality between the sexes and freedom for all."[3] Similarly, a Swiss federal court, ruling against a teacher who wanted to wear the *hijab* to class, argued that "it is difficult to reconcile the wearing of a headscarf with the principle of gender equality—which is a fundamental value of our society enshrined in a specific provision of the Federal constitution."[4] Feminists in France and elsewhere have made similar arguments, perhaps epitomized by Elisabeth Badinter, who maintains that for women, "the headscarf is a terrible symbol of submission," associated with the "religious imperialism" that the secular state was designed to combat.[5] It is as if the arrival of secularism had solved the problem of sexual difference in history, bringing in its wake an end to what Tocqueville referred to as "the oldest of all inequalities, that between man and woman."[6] From this perspective, religious communities and societies are relics of another age, and veiled women, with their sexuality under wraps, are the quintessential sign of backwardness.

In this chapter I call into question the simple oppositions—modern/traditional, secular/religious, sexually liberated/sexually oppressed, gender equality/patriarchal hierarchy, West/East—from three different perspectives. The first has to do with the history of secularization, which I argue makes it clear that the equal status of women and men was not a primary concern for those who moved to separate church and state. Here, we might find in my typos an unconscious association that takes the form of a metonymic slippage: from secularism to sexism. The second perspective is the notion of individual agency that so often informs discussions of the emancipatory effects of secularism. We could say that my unwitting substitution of an *x* for a *c* marks as a mistake the elision of the secular and the sexually liberated—their assumed synonymity. And finally I argue that, from a psychoanalytic perspective, secularism has not resolved the difficulties that sexual difference poses for social and political organization. It could be that the very trouble we have in pronouncing the title of this chapter—"Sexularism"—captures something of the persistent problem of trying to reconcile sexual difference and gender equality, even in a so-called secular age.

History

The French Revolution is one of the founding moments of modernity: a product of the Enlightenment, a political transformation of gigantic proportions that substituted the rule of reason—and thus of law—for the superstitions of priests and the power of kings. Among the many processes launched by the elected representatives of the people was secularization. The mighty Roman Catholic Church in its French incarnation was nationalized by the state; priests who swore allegiance to the French Republic became the state's paid agents, while the clergy who did not swear were left to perform illicit masses underground; and signs of religious devotion (statues of saints, crucifixes, church bells) were replaced by allegorical embodiments of secular concepts (liberty, fraternity, equality, the social contract, philosophy, reason, virtue) in idealized classical forms. Even words of consolation were laicized in at least one cemetery: "Death is eternal sleep" denied all possibility of a heavenly afterlife. The revolutionaries organized festivals as substitutes for religious pageants; artists, musicians, writers, actors, and playwrights were mobilized in a huge propaganda effort aimed at instilling allegiance to the new order of things.

One example was the Fête of Unity and Indivisibility, orchestrated by the painter Jacques-Louis David and the composer François-Joseph Gossec on August 10, 1793. Its five stations took citizens through what the art historian Madelyn Gutwirth describes as a "pseudo-masonic procession of initiation."[7] The Fountain of Regeneration was at the first station, that of nature. Gutwirth describes it on the basis of a print in the Bibliothèque Nationale: "A huge statue of an Egyptian Hathor, seated between her two mastiffs, was erected, from whose breasts—chastely covered by her crossed arms—streamed the milk (we recall it was merely water) of rebirth. . . . [T]he immediate benefactors of her largesse [were] the distinguished legislators of the state, lined up before her, to make symbolic consumption of her bounty."[8] Gutwirth provides an incisive psychoanalytic reading of this scene and of many other instances she cites that were marked by an abundance of breast imagery (especially, but not only, during the Revolution's Jacobin phase):

> The sheer sterile aridity of this derivative, trumped-up breast imagery, divorced from its real subtexts both of transcendence—the ties linking sex, birth, death, and eternity—and of the warmth of fleshly human affinities, mark it as a fetishistic phenomenon. In the midst of the Jacobins' struggle to assert human equality, its men insisted to the last on the premise that signs of otherness can be exploited to express an ideal. A desperate insistence on the repetition of the forms of sexual dimorphism of other ages characterizes its major representations. The Revolution divorces the breast from its context; that is, from the women's powers of intention, heart, and mind. The Revolutionaries' preoccupation with the breast is the indicator of a gender split in the new republican mentality so deep as to defy repair. Women's foreignness to republican culture was reified by its representation. Increasingly locked into repetitive verbal and visual structures, by the era of Thermidor the new French political culture had definitively thrown away all grounds for anything akin to parity between women and men, even in difference.[9]

Looking at several other representations, especially a popular image of *Republican France Offering her Breasts to all Frenchmen*, which she labels a "democratic pinup," Gutwirth concludes that the "figuration of the breast" no longer serves as it once did, as a sign of universal charity; instead "it has been restored as an adjunct to male eroticism."[10]

If Gutwirth cites what might be seen as the more benign (because abstract) representations of the feminine, Richard Cobb provides evidence from reports of the work of the "people's armies." He writes that the de-Christianizing campaigners "at times came near to misogyny" in their association of women with priests. To take just one of the many examples he offers, a commissioner was reported to have "thundered against fanaticism, and in particular against women, who were more easily seduced by it; he said that the Revolution had been made by men, and the women should not be allowed to make it backtrack."[11]

I have cited Gutwirth and Cobb because their material permits me to join the two themes of secularism and gender equality. Contrary to so many claims, I want to argue that not only is there no necessary connection between them, but that the equality that secularism promises has always been troubled by sexual difference, by the difficult—if not impossible—task of assigning ultimate meaning to bodily differences between women and men. Those who insist on the superiority of secularism compared to religion, as if the two categories were in eternal opposition rather than discursively interdependent, tell a story of the evolution of modernity. From their perspective, there may be interruptions and distractions, setbacks and confusions, but the secular ideal—synonymous with progress, emancipation, and freedom from the strictures of religiously based traditionalism—inevitably prevails in the end. Such is the view propounded by the philosopher Charles Taylor in *A Secular Age*. Discussing "Locke's egalitarian imaginary," Taylor notes that it was "at the outset profoundly out of synch with the way things in fact ran. . . . Hierarchical complementarity was the principle on which people's lives effectively operated—from kingdom . . . to family. We still have some lively sense of this disparity in the case of the family, because it is really only in our time that the older images of hierarchical complementarity between men and women are being comprehensively challenged. But this is a late stage in a 'long march' process."[12]

Of course, the evidence I have offered from the French Revolution

could be used to substantiate this "long march" view of things. Indeed, it has been argued that after a rocky start, due to remnants of
law and custom from the ancien régime, the notion of individual
rights spread from groups of elite men to all members of society. The
pace of progress was uneven but inevitable, in this view, even if it took
centuries to come to fruition.[13]

I want to challenge this story and suggest that the "long march"
view is, instead, a feature of the discourse of secularism. I agree with
Talal Asad who, disputing Taylor's Hegelian teleology, characterizes
the "long march" story as a myth of liberalism: "What has often been
described as the political exclusion of women, the propertyless, colonial subjects in liberalism's history can be re-described as the gradual
extension of liberalism's incomplete project of universal emancipation."[14] Calling for a critique of the idealized secular in the form of a
genealogy of secularism, Asad comments that "the secular is neither
singular in origin nor stable in its historical identity, although it works
through a series of particular oppositions," among them the political
and the religious, the public and the private.[15] To this list I would add
the opposition between reason and sex. In the idealized version of
secularism, the consignment of the passions to a private sphere makes
reasonable conversation and conduct possible in the realms of the
public and the political. To put it another way, the hierarchies of the
private sphere are the referents for organizing the public sphere.

In this idealized secularism, there is a link between religion and sex
that needs further exploration, not because the religious and the
erotic are one (though that may be something others want to discuss), but because secularization in the Christian lands of the West
proceeds by defining religion as a matter of private conscience, in the
same way and at the same time that it privatizes familial and sexual
matters. Of course, the public/private distinction was not a clear one,
but rather a hypothetical boundary requiring constant regulation by
state authorities. The family was deemed a private institution, the site
of emotion and intimacy, and as such it was also considered key to
public order. Laws defined the terms of marriage, divorce, inheri-
tance, and what counted as acceptable sexual practices, even though
these were thought to belong to the province of religious moral
teaching. Religious institutions were subjected to similar regulations

by the secularizing states of Western Europe. Indeed, one scholar has argued: "The historical relationship between family and state sovereignty . . . becomes a source of continual entanglements between religion and politics."[16]

The public/private distinction operated within the family and the state to establish citizenship along the lines of sexual difference. When reason became the defining attribute of the citizen and when abstraction enabled the interchangeability of one individual citizen for another, passion was assigned not just to the marital bed (or the chambers of the courtesan), but to the sexualized body of the woman. So it was that both domestic harmony and public disorder were figured in female form; the "angel in the house" and the unruly *pétroleuse* are two sides of the same coin.[17] Masculinity was defined in contrast to both of these representations: men were the public face of the family and the reasoning arbiters of the realm of the political. Their existence as sexual beings was at once secured in relation to women and displaced onto them. The public/private demarcation so crucial to the secular/religious divide rested on a vision of sexual difference that legitimized the political and social inequality of women and men.

It is not simply that religion and sex are to private conscience what politics and citizenship are to public activity. They are intertwined categories because in the process of secularization in the West, women (the embodiment of sex) were—as shown in the French examples I began with—usually associated with religion and religious belief. Indeed, the feminization of religion was a phenomenon that drew anxious comment from American Protestants during the nineteenth century; the susceptibility of women to priestly influence was long used to justify denying them the vote in the Catholic countries of Europe; and women's role as the bearers and embodiments of tradition, including customary religious practices, created dilemmas for leaders of revolutions of national liberation in the twentieth century. The discursive assignment of women and religion to the private sphere was not—in the first articulations of the secular ideal—about the regulation by religion of female sexuality. Rather, feminine religiosity was seen as a force that threatened to disrupt or undermine the rational pursuits that constitute politics; like feminine sexuality, it was excessive, transgressive, and dangerous. So, to return for a minute to those French revolutionary armies, we have this vehement comment from a *repré-sentant en mission* in the Gers: "And you, you bloody bitches, you are their [the priests'] whores, particularly those who attend their bloody masses and listen to their mumbo-jumbo."[18]

The danger of feminine sexuality was not taken as a religious phenomenon but as a natural one. Secularists removed God as the ultimate intelligent designer and put nature in his place. They saw nature not as an outside force, but as an essence that could be inferred from all living things, humans included. To act in accordance with nature was to fulfill one's inherent capacities, and for humans these were determined by sex. The major political theorists from the seventeenth century on assumed that human political actors were men. They did not cite religious explanations for women's exclusion from active citizenship; instead, they pointed to the qualities that followed from the incontestable biological difference of sex. Thomas Laqueur has documented the ways in which eighteenth-century medical writing informed political theory: "The truths of biology had replaced divinely ordained hierarchies or immemorial custom as the basis for the creation and distribution of power in relations between men and women."[19] Men were individuals, owning that property in the self that enabled them to conclude contracts—including the founding article of political society, the social contract. And men could be abstracted from their physical and social embodiment: that was what the abstract individual was about. Women, in contrast, were dependent, a consequence of the dedication of their bodies to reproduction; they did not own themselves and thus were not individuals. And there was no abstracting women from their sex. When the French revolutionaries who attempted to domesticate the Catholic church banned women from political meetings and active citizenship, it was on the grounds of biology: "The private functions for which women are destined by their very nature are related to the general order of society; social order results from the differences between man and woman. Each sex is called to the kind of occupation which is fitting for it; its action is circumscribed within this circle which it cannot break through, because nature, which has imposed these limits on man, commands imperiously and receives no law."[20]

The point is that both at the originary moments of secularism (in its democratic or republican forms) and also well into its history, women were not considered men's political equals.[21] The difference of sex was taken to be a legitimate ground for inequality. As Carole Pateman puts it succinctly: "Sexual difference is political difference; sexual difference is the difference between freedom and subjection."[22] The US Constitution included an establishment clause in 1791, but women did not get the right to vote until 1920. The French Revolution subordinated church to state for a time; the law that enacted today's *laïcité* was not passed until 1905; and women were enfranchised only in 1944. Although the United States and France followed different paths in the regulation and privatization of religion, the outcome for women was the same.

In these countries, although women are now voters, there are still only small proportions of them in legislative bodies—today women account for some 19 percent of the deputies in the French National Assembly and about 17 percent in the US House of Representatives.[23] Moreover, even after enfranchisement, civil and family laws remained on the books that placed women in a dependent, inferior position, despite their formal legal rights. In the United States, although there were statutes that recognized married women's independent contractual rights, well into the twentieth century judges continued to apply common-law notions that defined marriage in terms of a wife's domestic service to her husband.[24] Similarly, in France, provisions of the civil and criminal code dating from the Napoleonic era remained in effect until they were revised in the period 1965–75. Until then, husbands controlled their wives' wages, decided whether or not they could work for pay, and determined unilaterally where the family would live. Married women could not have individual bank accounts, and their sexual transgressions were punished more severely than men's. For example, women's adultery warranted imprisonment, while men were subject to criminal action only if they introduced their mistresses into the family domicile. In these countries, the glass ceiling was evident everywhere, even in a time of changing sexual norms—no more so than during the financial turmoil of 2008–10, as men in dark suits and ties gathered around tables in boardrooms and government offices to devise a fix for the latest crisis of capitalism.

If all of what I have described so far can still be accommodated by the "long march" story, other factors make it more difficult. The formal enfranchisement of women did not end their social subordination. Even when, after years of feminist agitation, women in these democracies won the right to vote, references to a biologically mandated sexual division of labor were used to place them in a socially subordinate relationship to men. In many countries, the enfranchisement of women was conceived of as the extension of group, not individual, rights. The formal rights of the citizen for women did not translate into social and economic equality; citizenship did not change the norms that established women as different. They might gain formal political equality, but substantively—in the family, the marketplace, and the political arena—they were hardly equal. The political theorist Wendy Brown puts it this way: "Women's formal political equality is neither the sign nor the vehicle of their integration. To the contrary, that equality is founded in a presumption of difference organized by a heterosexual division of labor and underpinned by a heterosexual familial structure, all of which attenuate the need for tolerance and at the same time underscore the differences between formal and substantive equality."[25] If in recent years there has been a sexual revolution— what Eric Fassin refers to as an extension of democratic logic to the realm of sex and sexuality—this has yet to translate into equality across the board.[26] Indeed, it is striking that the very same French politicians who in 1999 ridiculed feminist demands for a law granting equal access to elective office for women and men ("It's a concert of vaginas," one senator commented, on hearing feminist demands), became great advocates of women's equality when it came to talking about Muslims in 2003.[27] It is precisely the remaining gender (and other) discriminations in secular societies that are obscured when secularism and religion are categorically contrasted. That is because gender—the assignment of normative roles to men and women—is most often taken as an entirely social phenomenon; the psychic dilemmas presented by sexual difference are not taken into account. When they are, we may find that processes of secularization have, historically, served to intensify rather than relieve the dilemmas that attend sexual difference.

In order to see whether or not this is the case, we have to approach the history of secularization not as a singular, evolutionary process, but with a series of questions that separate its many strands. There are a number of different histories that need to be written from this alternative perspective, but they all aim at eliciting the changing meanings of the term "secularism" as well as its relationship to sex and sexuality. One such history has to do with state formation in the West and the state's contest for power with religious institutions—the most literal aspect of the process of secularization. Here the effects of privatizing religion need to be thought of in relation to the privatization of the domestic sphere and to the ways in which states regulated these domains. A second has to do with the dissemination of secular ideals elsewhere: what they were, and how they became a template for modernity outside the West. A third has to do with sexuality: changing representations of male and female, masculinity and femininity; and the political and social histories of the relations between men and women. A fourth would consider demography, the way concerns about rising or falling birthrates moved the rulers of nations to pursue policies directed at regulating marriages and defining what counted as a family. A fifth would take science, medicine, and technology into account and ask how developments in these areas made possible changes in norms governing sex and sexuality. A sixth would look at economic development, bringing together the state, the market, and gender, especially the way theories of political economy envision and so implement sexual divisions of labor in the market and the family. These different strands, of course, intersect and influence one another, but not in the way the "long march" story imagines. Rather, the intersections are disparate, discontinuous, and contingent; they don't all fall into line at the same time and in the same way. That is why we need histories to illuminate and account for them; only then will a genealogy of secularism be possible. When we have such a genealogy, we will have revealed the very recent origin of the discourse that takes sexual emancipation to be the fruit of secularism. This discourse is located in our particular historical context, one in which the hyperbolic language of a "clash of civilizations" and a "crisis" of secularism has come to characterize what ought to be more-nuanced discussions about the complex relationships within and between Islam and the West.

More History

In this chapter I cannot begin to illustrate what the genealogy of secularism would look like, but I can offer some starting points for conceptualizing it.

Secularization The history of secularization in the Christian West is tied to the emergence of the nation-state and to the separation of politics from religion. Whether the theorists of what we now call secularism and the politicians who sought to implement it aimed to place denominational struggles outside the realm of national and international politics, to deny political authority to ecclesiastical leaders, or to subordinate the power of churches to state control, they addressed the relationship between the institutions of church and state with little reference to the relationships between women and men. A case in point is the French law of 1905 that separated church and state, one of the exemplary laws of modern European secularism. The law never mentioned gender at all, as it spelled out the boundaries of separation between church and state. Liberty of individual conscience is the first article of the law of separation; the second pertains to the republic's refusal to recognize or underwrite any particular religion. There are rules prohibiting religious icons on public monuments; rules about paying chaplains for their services in schools, hospitals, and prisons; attempts to define what constitutes a recognizable religion; and the creation of a *police des cultes* to enforce the provisions of the law. As the state brings religious institutions under its control, it often refers to the Conseil d'Etat for advisory judgments. (The Conseil d'Etat is the highest administrative court in France, whose task is to deal with the legality of actions taken by public bodies.) For eighty years, none of the judgments relating to the law of 1905 concerned gender equality, while other rulings of the Conseil did refer to the status of women and to discrimination against them, focusing on the different institutional contexts—workplace, school, university—involved. Gender equality comes into focus in relation to secularization for the first time in 1987 when, seeking to bring French practice into conformity with the European Convention's prohibition of sex discrimination, the Conseil decides that Catholic women's religious orders must be treated in the same way as those of men.[28] Even when offering its first opinion about the legitimacy of banning Islamic head scarves in schools in 1989, the Conseil did not raise the question of gender equality. Rather, it framed its decision in terms of threats to the public order and proselytizing in a public school. (In 1989 it found neither to be in evidence.) In 2004, on the eve of passage of the head scarf ban, a report by the Conseil noted that its previous decisions had been less influenced than they now would be by "questions linked to Islam and to the place and status of Muslim women in society."[29] The question of women's equality as a feature of the separation of church and state was a new one for this body that had been offering guidance for nearly a century on the meanings of the law of 1905. It came up only in the context of heated debates about the place of North African immigrants in French society.

Imperialism In the process of Western secularization, the status of women became a concern of modernity in association with imperialist adventures. Colonial powers often justified their conquests in terms that made the treatment of women—their segregation and sexual exploitation, but not their equality—an index of civilization. Well before women won the vote in France, descriptions of life in North Africa stressed the superiority of French gender relations compared to those of the Arabs. Julia Clancy-Smith describes it this way: "In the imperial imagination, behind the high walls of the Arab household, women suffered oppression due to Islamic laws and customs. As the colonial gaze fixed progressively upon Muslim women between 1870 and 1900, Islam was moved by many French writers from the battlefield into the bedroom."[30] In Algeria, as early as the 1840s, one way of distinguishing between what the French took to be the superior Kabyles (who were singled out to be aides to colonial administrators because they were seen as more like the French) and the Arabs was the two groups' treatment of women. Paul Silverstein describes the construction of what he calls the "myth" of Kabyle superiority this way: "According to scholars, the Kabyles continued to hold their women in high respect; Kabyle women were masters of the household, went in public unveiled, and generally 'have a greater liberty than Arab women'; they count more in society."[31] And at the height of the Algerian war for independence (1954–62), the wives of French colonial administrators organized women's associations aimed at freeing native women from the constraints of Islamic law. A ceremony in 1958 that involved the unveiling of Muslim women was meant to display the civilizing mission in action; France was not, as the nationalists claimed, an oppressor, but—in this scenario—a liberator.[32] The removal of the veil proved it. We can see here the similarities to justifications offered by the Bush administration for the war in Afghanistan—as a mission of liberation from "Islam" for women there—even as it pushed an agenda that compromised hard-won rights for women at home, often in the name of Christian religious truth.

Algerian nationalists, many also committed to some form of modernity, found it hard to offer their own form of emancipation to women while resisting the imposition of colonial ideals. Frantz Fanon, who was a member of the National Liberation Front, commented: "The tenacity of the occupier in his enterprise to unveil the women, to make of them an ally in the work of cultural destruction, had the effect of strengthening traditional patterns of behavior."[33] Fanon's essay "Algeria Unveiled"—struggling as it does with the need to insist on the integrity of a traditional Algerian culture against French attempts to absorb it, on the one hand, and the desire to modernize that culture, on the other hand—reveals the ways in which the pressure of contingent historical forces shape political and social outcomes.[34] Fanon may have thought that participating in the revolution would somehow raise women to men's level, but in fact independence did not bring about an egalitarian sharing of political responsibilities between women and men.[35] And the confusion about how to nationalize secular modernity remained a key aspect of politics for several decades. Those familiar tropes of the danger of women's religious attachments and the need to rein in their zeal—implicitly if not explicitly understood as sexual—were evident in forms specific to Algeria's history. They took another turn during the civil war in the early 1990s, when resurgent Islamist forces insisted on women's religious practices (embodied in the wearing of the veil) as a way of containing female sexuality and so of resisting Western materialism.

Exporting Modernity Exporting secularism as a product of modernity did not only exist under the aegis of colonial domination. In nineteenth-century Iran, Afsaneh Najmabadi argues, influences from the West led to anxiety about sex and masculine sexuality. Well before the shah's reforms in the twentieth century, "the modernist project of female emancipation—centered on the desirability of heterosocialization, unveiling women and encouraging them to socialize with men, and transforming marriage from a sexual contract to a romantic one —was premised on (and productive of) the disavowal of male homoeroticism. It was also pushed for eradication of same-sex practices among males."[36] Emancipation did not guarantee liberation, since the romantic marital contract still assumed a division of labor in which the home and its private functions were the woman's domain, while the public world of politics was the man's.

Lest these patterns be associated solely with liberalism, the Russian Revolution offers another kind of example. After the Bolsheviks came to power, women were granted complete civil, legal, and electoral equality, yet they remained secondary figures in the Communist Party and the government. They had greater economic opportunity than in the past, to be sure, but although women were encouraged to join the workforce, they were rarely found in top administrative or leadership positions. In iconic representations, the secular, rational, and physically potent young male worker stood for the revolution and the future, while the religious, superstitious "baba"—the old woman wearing a babushka—embodied its antithesis. Writing in 1978, the historian Richard Stites reported that Alexandra Kollantai had complained in 1922 that "the Soviet state was run by men and women were to be found only in subordinate positions." "And so it has remained," he concluded, "for the most part until this day."[37]

Agency

In definitions of secularism, the idea of equality is often linked to the autonomous agency of individuals, the preeminent subjects of secularism. They are depicted as freely choosing, immune to the pressures that traditional communities bring to bear on their members.

Thus, Riva Kastoryano defends the ban on Islamic head scarves in French public schools by invoking the need to protect women's autonomy from politically motivated religious authorities: "Law alone cannot help to liberate the individual—especially when the individual is a woman—from community pressures that have become the common rule in concentrated areas like *banlieues* in France. Still, such a law is important for liberating Muslims from Islam as a political force that weighs on Muslim migrant communities wherever they are settled."[38] Like many French secularists, she assumes that communal pressures are always negative forces, and that the only reason a woman would wear a head scarf is because she is forced to.

In fact, where there has been testimony from women in head scarves, their emphasis has been on choice, on their religiously in-spired individual agency. And in the more general debates about religion and secularism, historians have reminded those feminists who equate religion, patriarchy, and the subordination of women that the first wave of feminism drew on deeply held religious principles for its arguments. Indeed, it was white Protestant women who staffed the temperance, abolition, peace, and purity movements, gaining a space in public life as voices of Christian morality.[39] Their arguments rested on biblical passages and on their interpretations of theological texts. Second-wave feminism often forgets this fact in its antireligious, secu-lar emphasis. The historical insight to be gained here is not an evolu-tionary one—feminism did not evolve from religious to secular—but a contextual one: what distinguished the eighteenth- and nineteenth-century movements from the late-twentieth-century ones?

One of the interesting things about recent scholarship on religion has been its critical examination of the nature of religious agency, some of which has been conducted in the light of theoretical work on the constitution of subjects. The writings of the historian of religion Phyllis Mack on Quaker women in eighteenth-century England and of the anthropologist Saba Mahmood on women in pietistic Islamic sects in late twentieth-century Egypt both in different ways call into question the secular, liberal concept of agency as "the free exercise of self-willed behavior," the expression of a previously existing self.[40] Mack argues that in order to understand the extraordinary actions undertaken by Quaker women, "we need a conception of agency in which autonomy is less important than self-transcendence and in which the energy to act in the world is generated and sustained by a prior act of personal surrender."[41] In contrast, Mahmood suggests that "agentival capacity is entailed not only in resistance to norms, but in the multiple ways one inhabits those norms."[42] She reminds us of Foucault's definition of subjectivation: "The very processes and conditions that secure a subject's subordination are also the means by which she becomes a self-conscious identity and agent."[43] Foucault analyzed liberal subjects in these terms; Mahmood suggests that the definition also applies to religious subjects, and this leads her to a strong critique of the insistence on individual autonomy in some secular feminist emancipatory discourse.

Mack explores the Christian paradox of freedom in servitude to God. She writes that Quaker women "defined themselves as instruments of divine authority," who found in self-transcendence the "freedom to do what [was] right."[44] She continues: "The contradiction between the ideal of self-transcendence and the cultivation of a competent self was resolved by turning the energies of the individual outward, in charitable impulses toward others."[45] In contrast, Mahmood maintains that the pietistic Islamic women she studied did not see their religious practice as a means of expressing a self, but of embodying a virtuous life, one that aspired to attain the ethical standards of the "historically contingent discursive traditions in which they [were] located."[46] For some Muslims, Talal Asad notes, this tradition posits "a collective body of Muslims bound together by their faith in God and the Prophet—a faith that is embodied in prescribed forms of behavior."[47]

These traditions, according to Mahmood, are not throwbacks to the past, but "modern," and they need to be understood as such. "The relation between Islamism and liberal secularity," she writes, "is one of proximity and coimbrication rather than of simple opposition or . . . accommodation; it therefore needs to be analyzed in terms of the historically shifting, ambiguous, and unpredictable encounters that this proximity has generated."[48] Mack refuses to position her Quakers against the secular Enlightenment; rather, she says that there was "a new kind of psychic energy; a spiritual agency in which liberal notions of free will and human rights were joined to religious notions of individual perfectability, group discipline, and self-transcendence, and in which energy was focused not on the individual's interior state but on the condition of other deprived groups."[49] Eighteenth-century Quakers operated within a discourse of individual choice, while twentieth-century Muslims defined their practice in terms of community.

Whether addressing themselves to the needs of others, or subsuming themselves to a set of ethical requirements, these religious women acted within a set of normative constraints. Neither Mack nor Mahmood denies that gender inequality is a feature of these religious movements; indeed, Mahmood acknowledges her own initial repugnance for the "practices of the mosque movement . . . that seemed to circumscribe women's subordinate status within Egyptian society."[50] But she goes on to insist on the importance of understanding not only what is involved in the social conservatism of piety movements, but also the sources of our own secular feminist desire to condemn them as instances of forced subordination or false consciousness before we understand what they are about: "By tracing . . . the multiple modalities of agency that informed the practices of the mosque participants, I hope to redress the profound inability within current feminist political thought to envision valuable forms of human flourishing outside the bounds of a liberal progressive imaginary."[51]

In the heat of the controversies over head scarves, less attention has been paid to the explanations by women who wear them than to the critics who condemn them as a sexist sign. Since they take the sign to have only one meaning, the critics see no need to ask women why they cover their heads; moreover, any answer that disputes their interpretation is dismissed as false consciousness. There's a kind of reverse fundamentalism at play here, with secularists insisting on their perception of it as the single truth about the veil. "I am a feminist and I am allergic to the head scarf," a French teacher tells a Muslim student, as she orders her to remove her hijab.[52] When the girl replies that she has chosen to wear it against the wishes of her parents, the teacher tells her that "in removing your head scarf, you will return to normality." "What does that mean?" the girl asks. "What is normal in a class where students are allowed to wear dreadlocks? That is apparently normal, but not my head scarf."[53]

This kind of outspoken challenge is an indication of a certain agency: a strong assertion of the right to have one's religion recognized as a continuing aspect of self-construction—even if that self has been given over to, or realized through, submission to God.[54] The various testimonies offered by young women in head scarves invoke the theme of choice to explain their turn to what Asad calls embodied forms of prescribed behavior. This is partly strategic, since the discourse of liberal individualism is the dominant one in secular nations. But it is also a way of challenging that discourse, by linking choice not with emancipation but with a decision to submit. Here are two examples from France: "It's my choice, after all, if I don't want to show off my body."[55] "I wear the veil to submit to God—and I am totally responsible for my submission—but that also means I submit myself to no one else, even my parents. . . . I give myself to God and this God promises to protect and defend me. So those who want to try to tell me what to do, to hell with them."[56] And the *New York Times* recounted the story of Havva Yilmaz, a Turkish girl who, against the wishes of her parents, dropped out of school rather than remove the head scarf she had chosen to wear at age sixteen. "Before I decided to cover, I knew who I was not," she explained. "After I covered, I finally knew who I was."[57] The sociologist Nilüfer Göle says that what is at stake in comments like this one is the personal appropriation and reversal of a sign of what modernity sees as inferiority and a sign of women's oppression—in this case, the head scarf: "It expresses the exteriorization and the wish to turn the stigma into a sign of power and distinction for [Muslim] women."[58]

The defense of their right of religious expression has led many of these women to public activism, but not the kind usually associated with Islamist radicals who seek to impose their way of doing things on everyone else. Neither is there an endorsement of state-mandated covering for women, as in Saudi Arabia or Iran. Rather, the campaigns protest the forms of discrimination that the women experience in their countries—a discrimination that takes the head scarf as its object but is also about religious, ethnic, social, and economic difference. The women's goal is not to force everyone to do as they do, but to be recognized as legitimate members of a national community. In Turkey, Yilmaz led a movement to end the ban on head scarves in universities. "How can I be part of a country that does not accept me?" she asked. Although an attempted revision of the law by the prime minister was overruled by the Turkish Constitutional Court in June 2008, Yilmaz and her friends vowed to continue: "If we work together, we can fight it."[59] The Collectif des Féministes pour l'Egalité, founded in France in 2004, affirmed the right to wear or not to wear a head scarf; dedicated itself to the fight against sexist discrimination; and refused any single model of emancipation:[60] "We fight against the obligatory veil and against obligatory unveiling, for the right to have our heads uncovered or covered; it is the same fight: the fight for freedom of choice and, more precisely, for the right of each woman to dispose of her body as she wishes."[61] These are recognizable liberal democratic values—freedom of choice and women's control of their bodies—placed in the service of embodied forms of religious observance. Said one of the members of the Collectif, "I am a French woman of Western culture and the Muslim religion."[62]

The message here is clearly mixed: discourses of religious devotion and embodied ethical deportment combine with assertions of modernist notions of individual rights and pluralist democracy. They are as susceptible to change as any other discourses. Although the fight is about religious expression in public places, the neutrality of the state is assumed. Indeed, bans on head scarves are taken to be a violation of state neutrality and of the citizen's freedom of religious conscience. There is also no tolerance for the argument that the state must protect women from religious conservatives who would force them to veil. These young women (and most of them are young) consider that to be a form of paternalism in contradiction to principled commitments to equality; it is as objectionable in its way as state regulations that would mandate wearing the veil.

The argument against state paternalism was offered in 2005 in a case before the Grand Chamber of the Council of Europe (*Şahin v. Turkey*) in an eloquent dissent by one of the judges, Françoise Tulkens of Belgium. The majority upheld the Turkish court's ruling that the ban on head scarves in universities was consistent with the state's secular values and with the equality before the law of women and men. Judge Tulkens disagreed, pointing out that no connection between the ban and sexual equality had been demonstrated by the majority:

> The applicant, a young adult university student, said—and there is nothing to suggest that she was not telling the truth—that she wore the headscarf of her own free will. In this connection, I fail to see how the principle of sexual equality can justify prohibiting a woman from following a practice which in the absence of proof to the contrary, she must be taken to have freely adopted. Equality and non-discrimination are subjec-

tive rights which must remain under the control of those who are entitled to benefit from them. "Paternalism" of this sort runs counter to the case law of the Court, which has developed a real right to personal autonomy. Finally, if wearing the headscarf really was contrary to the principle of the equality of men and women in any event, the State would have a positive obligation to prohibit it in all places, whether public or private.[63]

It is precisely in defense of a certain vision of individual agency that Judge Tulkens and others I have cited protest state bans on head scarves. But this is a vision that—implicitly in Tulkens's dissent, explicitly in the comments of young women in hijab—acknowledges a distinction between self-governance and autonomy, a distinction that Asad associates with the Islamic *umma*: "The sharia system of practical reason morally binding on each faithful individual, exists independently of him or her. At the same time, every Muslim has the psychological ability to discover its rules and to conform to them."[64] Submission, then, in this view of things, is—paradoxically—a choice freely made. That is the point of this ironic question from a woman protesting the French ban: "If my veil is a 'symbol of oppression,' must I then conclude that I'm oppressing myself?"[65]

Many of the women defending their right to wear a head scarf admit that not all covered women freely choose to wear it. But that is no different, they insist, from women who feel pressured by boyfriends or husbands to conform to the dictates of Western fashion, or—to take an extreme example—from prostitutes forced by their pimps to wear miniskirts and heavy makeup. There are a range of explanations for any woman's choice of clothing, so why insist on only one meaning for wearing the veil?[66]

Agency, then, is not the innate property of an abstract individual, but the attribute of subjects who are defined by—subjected to— discourses that bring them into being as both subordinate and capable of action. It follows that religious belief does not in itself deny agency; rather, it creates particular forms of agency whose meanings and history are not transparently signaled by the wearing of a veil. If one of those meanings has to do with the idea that women are subordinate to men, comments a Muslim woman, this is not a problem confined to Islam: "Male domination is so widespread, why is it more likely when a woman wears a veil? It's not an issue of the veil or of Islam, it's the relationship between men and women that's a relationship of domination."[67] From this perspective, Islam is but a variant on Tocqueville's "oldest of all inequalities," and secularism is not the antithesis of religion but instead provides a different framework within which to address the problem that sexual difference seems to pose for modern subjects.

Sexual Difference

These brief citations of very different histories contain a recurring theme: sexual difference, seen as a natural distinction rooted in physical bodies, is the basis for representing the alternatives between past and future, superstition and rationality, private and public. The irreconcilability of these options is underscored by linking them to women and men—a fundamental division that seems to admit of no ambiguity, even if the roles the sexes actually play don't fall so neatly into one category or another. To the extent that these representations assuage deeply rooted, even unconscious, anxieties, they secure the plausibility of the secular. To the extent that they structure the meanings of secularism, they feed into its normative expectations; indeed they contribute to the production of sexed secular subjects. In this area, the observations of psychoanalysis—which is, after all, a critical commentary on the rationalism of the secular—are useful. Indeed, it might be argued that the best theorizing we have of sexuality and sexual subjectivity in modern secular societies occurs in the writings of Freud and his followers.[68]

The enigma of sexual difference is at the heart of psychoanalytic theory. Despite norms that attempt to prescribe behaviors for men and women that are said to conform to their bodily requirements, confusion remains about the very issues that secularism supposedly laid to rest. The confusion is expressed in fantasy, but also in conflicting attempts to impose definitive meaning. How should we define the pleasure that liberal subjects are said to be free to enjoy? What is the relationship between individual rights and the operations of desire? Whose desire is at issue—Men's? Women's? Both? Neither?—in a sexual relationship? Is Lacan's comment that "there is no such thing as a sexual relationship" simply a pessimist's gloss on love, or an astute diagnosis of the asymmetry between male and female desire in modern societies?

Like Freud, Lacan begins with the assumption that psychic identities do not correspond to anatomical bodies: masculinity and femininity, male and female, are psychic positions rather than expressions of innate biological makeup. They are, moreover, not clearly defined ways of being, even if there are social norms that presume to offer irrefutable definitions. Instead, there is a gap between anatomy and its sexuation, and thus between psychic and social (or cultural) processes of subjectivation, the former casting doubt on the prescriptions of the latter. That gap—the lack of fit between physiology, sexuality, and desire—can never be closed, and it explains the recurring and perhaps perpetual difficulty of pinning down the meanings of sexual difference. Sexual difference is an intractable problem.

The problem is compounded by an asymmetry between the different sexual positions (male or female) that precludes a complementary, parallel, or even inverse relationship. When Lacan said that whatever position a subject ended up in precluded a relationship with another subject, he did not mean by this that people don't have sexual intercourse—of course they do. Rather, he meant—as Bruce Fink puts it—that there is "*no direct relationship* between men and women insofar as they are men and women. In other words, they do not 'interact' with each other as man to woman and woman to man. Something gets in the way of their having any such relationship; something skews their interactions."[69] That something is the phallus, the signifier of desire.

According to Lacan, the child's individuation is accompanied by an imagined loss of wholeness, of the time when all demands were satisfied by an Other whose attention focused exclusively on the child. Coming into language and separation from the primary parental figure (usually the mother) both involve a certain alienation, the loss of what seems in retrospect to have been the pleasure (jouissance) associated with total fulfillment. This imagined loss or lack is what Lacan means by castration. Desire is the impossible wish to recover the loss or replenish the lack; its signifier is the phallus.

Masculine and feminine subjects differ in their relationship to the phallus. The masculine subject is wholly defined in terms of symbolic castration, understood as the father's prohibition of the child's incestuous wish to reunite with his mother—a wish that nonetheless continues to animate his fantasies, and that he deflects onto other objects (referred to by Lacan as "object (a)"). The power of that wish comes from the belief that there can be an exception to castration: the symbolic father, the source of the prohibition, is imagined not to be governed by his own law, and this exception suggests the possibility that castration can be avoided or negated. Lacan puts this in terms of an antinomy, or contradiction: on the one hand all men are castrated; on the other hand, there is one who is not castrated, not limited by the law (this is the "phallic exception"). But if one is not castrated, there may be others (any of those who identify with the father)—or so the fantasy goes, holding out the possibility of plenitude or full presence to masculine subjects. In contrast, the feminine subject assumes that, like her mother, she is already castrated. She neither reacts to a prohibition, nor can she identify with an exception. Therefore, she does not share man's fantasy of attaining full presence.[70] But she is animated by desire, and this is articulated in relation to the phallus ("a woman generally gains access to the signifier of desire in our culture via a man or a 'masculine instance,' that is, someone who comes under the psychoanalytic category 'Men'")—but not entirely.[71] Lacan posits another jouissance for women that, at least partly, "escapes the reign of the phallus," but this is not generalizable in the way the male exception is.[72] Masculinity is thus associated with the universal (an all-encompassing wholeness, the possibility of identifying with the phallus), and femininity with the particular (no signifier of desire is equated with women; they are defined in their differences from it).

If we take Lacan's theorization of modern sexed subjects to be located in modernity's history, we can ask a series of questions that can be answered historically: How does the identification of masculinity with the universal and of femininity with the particular connect to secularism's ideas of public and private, to the abstractions of citizenship, and to the definition of women as "the sex"? Are these timeless attributes of sexual difference or the specific characteristics of secular subjects, which would mean the identifications are historically based patterns of psychic development? Are there unique ways in which secularism addresses sexual difference? Does it matter if God or nature or culture is the foundation on which the explanations for sexual difference rest? How does it matter? Are there particular approaches to sexuality that can be called "secular"? Are they necessarily linked to gender equality in its substantive as well as its formal implementation? Or is gender equality, paradoxically, undermined by psychic processes associated with secularism, which insist on the irreconcilable differences between men and women, the spheres that separate them? What have secularists meant by equality? How has this meaning changed over time? And what has equality signified in relation to psychic anxieties about the meanings of sexual difference? Thinking about sexual difference in this way—as an irritant to explanations that assume economic, social, and political practices are completely rational—lets us move beyond the emancipatory story that secularism has learned to tell about itself.

Conclusion

I am not arguing that there is no difference between what are called secular and religious societies in their treatment of women. Of course there are differences, differences that matter for the kinds of possibilities open to women (and men) in the course of their lives. But to what extent are the differences a matter of "secularism" or "religion"? When looked at historically, it is clear that the differences are not always as sharp as contemporary debates suggest (religious influences persist in societies called secular), and that the sharpness of the distinction works to obscure the continuing problems evident in so-called secular societies by attributing all that is negative to religion. This approach also assumes that, unlike secularism, religion is not affected by changing historical circumstances and is not itself a modern phenomenon, when of course it is. One of the big problems for secularism obscured in this way is the idea of equality—or, to put it more precisely, the idea of the relationship between equality and difference. What is the measure of equality in the face of difference? How can we reconcile the very different forms of equality—political, substantive, and subjective—and the fact that one does not necessarily guarantee the other? This is a problem that liberal secularism has struggled with in the course of its long history, not only in reference to women and men. One effort at resolution—the one we are now witnessing in dramatic form in relation to Islam—is the displacement of the problem onto unacceptable societies with other kinds of social organization. It is this displacement that I have called into question, insisting instead on a more nuanced and complex historical approach to the two supposedly antithetical concepts: the religious and the secular. Such an approach not only offers greater insight into both sides of the divide, but it also calls into question the divide itself, revealing its conceptual interdependence and the political work that it does. This then opens the way to thinking differently not only about others and about ourselves, but also about the nature of the relationship between us—the one that exists, and the alternative one we may want to construct.

5. French Seduction Theory

THE BICENTENNIAL of the French Revolution provided politicians and scholars with an opportunity not only to celebrate the inaugural chapter of the French Republic's history, but also to think anew about the meaning of national identity. Amid paeans to liberty, equality, and fraternity; critiques of Jacobinism; condemnations of the Terror; and revisions of previous histories of the entire event, there emerged an unprecedented appreciation of the legacy of absolutism and aristocracy. It came from a small group of influential Parisians clustered around the publishing house Gallimard, the journals *Le Débat* and *L'Esprit*, and the weekly *Le Nouvel Observateur*. In books and articles, they fashioned what might be called an ideology of aristocratic republicanism, which refused liberal notions of formal equality and democratic notions of social equality in the name of inherently unequal differences of sex. The supposedly natural attraction between men and women, best exemplified by seduction, was offered as a model for all forms of intercourse, a way of living happily with difference when there was no possibility for parity in the relationship between the parties.

The philosopher Philippe Raynaud describes seduction as "a particular form of equality."[1] And the historian Mona Ozouf, in a review of the literary historian Claude Habib's book on gallantry (dedicated to Ozouf), asks: "Is seduction a French art?" Her answer is unequivocally yes.[2] In her view, seduction has none of the negative connotations associated with nineteenth-century morality tales of innocent young women corrupted and then abandoned by their conniving male superiors. It has nothing to do with Freudian theories linking hysterical symptoms to repressed desire. Rather, seduction is a game of honor, marked by "sly and frivolous gaiety," in Habib's words.[3] To play is, above all, pleasurable.

This theory of seduction exploits a long-standing literary historical tradition that vaunted the aesthetic and erotic culture of the French nobility. By cleverly appealing to distinctive aspects of this culture as a model for all aspects of social and political life, Ozouf and her colleagues propose an alternative to what they take to be the dangers of democracy. Seduction offers not equality, but a naturalized, ahistorical version of inequality. Ozouf, insisting on its transcendent Frenchness, refers to it as *"la singularité française."*[4] Eric Fassin, criticizing this characterization, deems it "the sacralization of sexual difference . . . at the heart of the national project."[5]

For the advocates of aristocratic republicanism, seduction *à la française* became the answer both to domestic claims for social, economic, and political equality on the part of feminists, gay and lesbian activists, and Muslim immigrants and to alternative political systems elsewhere, whether based on individualism (as in the United States) or collectivism (as in totalitarian communist regimes). In all of these bad examples, the end result was said to be a leveling sameness. In contrast, by insisting on the play of difference between the sexes, the nationalist intellectuals kept things closer both to nature and to culture. The apparent contradiction between hierarchy (aristocracy) and equality (republicanism) was resolved by likening all difference to sexual difference. Seduction claimed to resolve the ideologically incoherent amalgam that was aristocratic republicanism; it sought to counter the leveling tendencies of democracy by an appeal to historical tradition. In this sense it functioned not as history, but as myth in Jacques Lacan's definition: "Myth is always a signifying system or scheme, which is articulated so as to support the antinomies of certain psychic relations."[6]

The myth of seduction challenges both feminist history and theory. It brutally dismisses the idea that inequality between the sexes is a problem to be remedied, and it offers a fantasized version of history, one that has little to do with the lived realities either of gender or power. It's not enough, though, to try to correct the factual record; more accurate history does not compete easily with the allure of fantasy. More useful, it seems to me, is to try to read analytically—psychoanalytically—in order to explore the political implications and commitments of this French theory of seduction.

Imagined Communities

The idea of a distinctive national character has a long history, and not only in France; it is part of the story of the emergence of nation-states. Nationalist ideologies are "invented traditions" in Eric Hobsbawm's terms, "imagined communities" according to Benedict Anderson.[7] They are constructed discursively in a variety of ways: in contrast with other nations whose differences establish the home country's superiority; by suppressing differences within the nation; by insisting on distinctive behavioral traits as marks of national membership; and by manufacturing histories that produce naturalized lineages as conclusive proof of the existence of a long-established national family. These histories are the stuff of what I have called "fantasy echoes" in chapter 2; they provide the scenes for the imaginative identification through which a new generation establishes its rootedness in the past.

The French myth of seduction is particularly interesting because it departs from the more typical representations of gender and family that have been used to talk about the organization of states and traits of national character. In the standard versions, the family is a model for the state, a hierarchy based on natural difference that justifies the preeminence of men as national leaders. Women are depicted as the embodiment of timeless tradition and culture's authenticity, while men are history's agents, moving things forward, their actions marking the stages in a nation's growth. If relations between the sexes are addressed, it is usually as a matter of procreation—what it takes to replenish the population in numbers that will contribute to prosperity and national well-being. Sex is discussed functionally, in terms of a strict division of reproductive labor: men's all-important contribution starts the process (and often names its end product), but it is women who bear, nurture, and raise the nation's children. From this follow the distinctions between public and private, political and domestic, active and passive, reason and passion. Sex—as the pursuit of desire, amorous play, and conjugal activity—remains in the realm of the private; it may be referred to obliquely and evoked metaphorically, but typically it is not considered a dimension of national character.

French seduction theory offers an entirely different scenario. It brings the play of sex to the fore as the defining attribute of gender relations; it concerns neither family nor children. It is governed not by law but by ritual; it depends not on formal regulations, but on a mutual understanding of the rules of play. Seduction serves no obvious social function, yet it becomes, in the writings of these nationalist intellectuals, a model for the workings of society. In their model, difference is treated as a field of play; the game is not one of sex war or, for that matter, class struggle. Conflict and coercion are absent from this vision of seduction. Instead, the different desires of women and men are given free rein. Scenes of the joyous pursuit of sexual pleasure invite readers' identification, stimulating their own desire to enact those roles and to imagine them as the basis for an alternative system of political relationships.

Those who tout seduction as a "singular" French trait argue that its aristocratic provenance does not contradict democratic values: "The difference between France and other democracies doesn't have to do with 'formal' equality or with 'real' equality; rather it comes from a certain economy of passion (*économie passionnelle*), which is expressed by a half-serious, half-ironic investment in roles reputed to be traditional."[8] Deeply embedded in national character—the fruit of a fortunate history, in which aristocratic manners were incorporated into republican practice—is "a special quality of irony that preserves that which is precious in the difference of the sexes without renouncing the requirement for rights and dignity."[9]

Eros Is Civilization

The starting point for the project might well have been the bicentennial issue of *Le Débat*, November–December 1989, in which several articles were devoted to a reconsideration of aristocratic principles, privileges, and customs. Raynaud contributed one on the role of women in aristocratic circles, "Les femmes et la civilité: aristocratie et passions révolutionnaires." His aim, he writes, is to provide "a certain rehabilitation of continental monarchies (aristocratic and absolutist, but civilized nonetheless) of which France is the classic model."[10] Briefly, he argues that French absolutism valued, indeed encouraged, a distinctive kind of civility that gave special recognition to women.

In her own contribution to this story, *Les mots des femmes: essai sur la singularité française*, Ozouf relies on Raynaud's argument. France, she claims, was the "ideal type of a civilized monarchy." At court, women enjoyed an unprecedented freedom: "They are the true motor of social life."[11] Like Raynaud, Ozouf uses the Scottish philosopher David Hume's comment about court life, where politeness and generosity were said to work to women's advantage: "In brief, the feminine art civilizes men from one end of the social scale to the other."[12]

Ozouf's book inspired Habib to pay tribute to French gallantry in her *Galanterie française*, which Ozouf describes as a "singular intercourse (*commerce*) between men and women" that had its heyday all too briefly, from the mid-seventeenth century into the eighteenth.[13] In an earlier book,[14] Habib writes of a time when, as yet another review by Ozouf puts it, women eagerly read Rousseau because they understood that he was on their side: "He saw woman as a being without power; but her weakness was her power, [she was] timid, but her modesty doubled her voluptuousness. It accentuated the dissymmetry of the sexes, but in order better to unite them."[15] Amorous consent, Habib insists, was free of crass calculation and had nothing to do with law or force; it was, rather, the ineffable expression ("mysterious" and gentle) of the "natural attraction" between the sexes. Men paid delicate tribute to women, slowly warming them to "virile desire." "This subtle game, played from first encounter to orgasm, involved learning to decode signs of agreement, to accept nuance and delay" is how the historian Alain Corbin (almost wistfully) describes the world of gallantry as portrayed by Habib.[16]

These manners were said not to be confined to the nobility, but trickled down into all levels of social life. Raynaud cites Hume to this effect: "In a civilized monarchy . . . there is a long chain of people dependent on one another which extends from the sovereign to the lowest of subjects; this dependence does not go so far as to threaten property or depress the people's spirit, but it inspires in them the desire to please their superiors and to model themselves on people of quality and on those with a distinguished education; from this it follows that the custom of politeness naturally originates in monarchies and courts."[17]

The myth, then, is this: in a time now past, there was a moment when manners and nature were in accord; when despite—or perhaps because of—the absolute control exercised by the monarchy, men and women could pursue and fulfill their erotic desires, unfettered by other considerations. "The taste for pleasure belongs to the nobility," Habib writes.[18] The absence of conflict is one of the central claims of the myth. Happy were the days at court when women liked being women and men liked being men, and when their attraction for one another took the form of polite and civil encounters. The repeated use of the word "civility" and its synonymity with civilization is key. Civility is (literally) the root of civilization and the mode of seduction—eros was civilization. Between seducer and seduced, there was "a delightful but ambiguous relationship."[19] Driven by desire, in pursuit of pleasure, the players regarded one another with mutual respect. Despite their reputed weakness, women gained considerable status from the desire of men to understand what women wanted; indeed, it was as objects of desire that women acquired agency in the game of seduction. In Habib's view, "the force of masculine desire is what constitutes feminine power."[20] Ozouf cites Renan, the architect of French nationalism, to make the point. The high tone of the nobility's discourse, the charm of its women, and its qualities of sympathy and spirituality, Renan writes, accounted for the "invincible superiority of France over all other nations."[21]

Somehow, according to these historians, what began as an aristocratic practice became inscribed in the nation's cultural DNA. Despite centuries of political and social transformation, traces of it endure today. Thus Ozouf writes: "If the model of fashionable and literate intercourse has disappeared in fact, it has not disappeared from our memory, nor—we must come back to this—from our national customs."[22] For Habib, the definitive proof of the persistence of these values, despite their steady erosion by the individualism of modern democracy, is the reaction of the French against the Islamic head scarf: "France is the only Western country to experience the veil as a problem."[23] Even in 2006, France was hardly the "only" country, but Habib's comment is strong evidence of the importance of seduction for thinking about French national identity in terms of sexual difference.

The Psychic Life of Power

Absolutism   Seduction had its ideal moment under the absolute monarchy, according to Raynaud and Habib. The age of Louis XIV was the time when the art was refined; the pursuit of erotic pleasure reached its apogee. It is important to note—a fact that these historians don't mention—that this was also the time of the loss of aristocratic political power as the monarchy consolidated its grip. Richelieu spoke of the need to reduce the pride of the great nobles, and this was done systematically by, among other things, attacking the political role that women had been allowed to play in the past. If there was a kind of gender equality in seduction, it did not translate into or reflect the world of politics.

Recent histories, especially those by Eliane Viennot, exhaustively document the decline in aristocratic women's power with the consolidation of absolutism.[24] Viennot is interested in women's access to political power, and she demonstrates the formidable role of queens, regents, mothers, and mistresses during the fifteenth, sixteenth, and seventeenth centuries. The Valois kings, she maintains, deliberately relied on noblewomen, who moved freely in court circles and had a recognized public place. This place was surely not universally accepted—as demonstrated by the famous *querelle des femmes* and several centuries of misogynist writing by disaffected bourgeois, provincial spokesmen, and foreigners. The "rediscovery" of the Salic law, which prohibited women from inheriting the throne, is another proof of the conflict that existed over women's political role in this early period. Still, Viennot argues, it wasn't until the Bourbon monarchs that noblewomen were definitively barred from politics. In an effort to consolidate monarchical power, noblewomen were then depicted as capricious, harebrained, and driven only by a desire for luxury and pleasure.[25]

But it was not only women who were denied power; noblemen were also cut off from politics and reduced to supplementary, often frivolous, roles at court. They were, in a sense, feminized—castrated —having lost the prerogatives that once defined their very being. In the regime of absolutism, all power was the king's; everyone else served to confirm his sovereignty. There was no confusion about who was in charge, who had the phallus—the signifier of all power. In this context, seduction was, for the nobility, not politics by other means, but an alternative game, a compensation for political impotence.

The dynamic of this seduction can be read in *Les liaisons danger-euses*, an epistolary novel published in 1782 by a minor noble with a military commission, Pierre-Ambroise-François Choderlos de Laclos. The novel shocked contemporaries, some of whom denounced it as scandalous and diabolical, even as it sold out printing after printing and was rapidly translated into several European languages. Some thought it a clever roman à clef, others an exaggerated portrait of the mores of the court. For us the interesting aspect of the novel is its portrayal of seduction as a contest between two ultimately impotent players.

The story of the Vicomte de Valmont and the Marquise de Mer-teuil is one of their repeated seductions of others, an erotic game that fuels the flirtation between them. There is no gentle commerce here, and the point of their game is to ruin the object of desire—whether male or female. Valmont writes to the Marquise to persuade her to humiliate her latest conquest: "He must be made to look publicly ridiculous and I'd like to repeat my request for you to do just that."[26] Sex is the ultimate, perhaps the only, form of power. The game, undeniably pleasurable, proceeds through deception, violence, and the cruel manipulation of others and of each other. But in the end, perhaps as an allegory of noble impotence, neither party gets what he or she wants; there is only endless play and death.

Valmont is the male predator women are warned to avoid, but Merteuil is his equal. She describes herself as "a self-made woman," who has figured out how to strategically avoid the degradation that follows from women's unequal position in the game of love.[27] Her account of herself is a reflection on the fate of her female contempo-raries: "In fact, in this mutual exchange of the bonds of love, to use the current jargon, only you men are able to decide whether to strengthen them or break them. We can consider ourselves lucky indeed, if, in your flighty way, you prefer to lie low rather than show off and are content merely to humiliate us by deserting us and not turn the woman you worshiped yesterday into today's victim!"[28] Merteuil describes herself as the exception, but she also can be read as a sign of noble castration more generally. Paired with Valmont, she reminds us that—in the world of real politics—he, too, is feminized. Their seductive play is, after all, the same: attractive, capricious, impossible to avoid, and dangerous when engaged. In this they perhaps imitate monarchical behavior, but there is a difference: neither has the phallus, which is the attribute of the king alone.

Seduction is conducted according to a code of manners; civility is the rule, even as strategies of conquest (often painful) are implemented. But the civility that Laclos depicts is a far cry from that evoked by Ozouf and Habib. It is a way of relating, to be sure, but it masks games of cruel deception, the strategies of the weak who want to appear to be strong. Dissimulation takes place under the cover of civility; women, warns the elderly Madame de Rosemonde, must not expect their passion to be reciprocated in kind; instead they must find their pleasure in the pleasure they give men: "A man enjoys the pleasure he feels, a woman the pleasure she bestows. This difference, so essential and so unnoticed, has however a very marked effect on their respective general behaviour. The pleasure of one partner is to satisfy his desires, that of the other is primarily to arouse them. For the man, pleasing is merely a means to succeed whereas for her it is success itself."[29] At once a reflection on the unequal relationships of the gendered players in the game of seduction, this advice can also be read as a commentary on the rules of politics under absolutism.

Republicanism If aristocratic seduction was defined by its relationship to absolutism, what does it mean to try to reconcile it with republicanism? This is a legitimate question, since Ozouf and her colleagues are not simply endorsing styles of erotic encounter (good manners, civility, pleasure in the chase), they are also insisting that seduction has important political implications. What might these be in the absence of an absolute ruler? Does anyone actually have the phallus when, as is the case in democracies, "the people" and "the nation" are abstractions? Can this potent symbol of sovereign power be shared?

In the origin stories told by democratic theorists, a band of brothers kills their father, ending his tyrannical rule and opening the way for shared governance.[30] But there remains ambiguity about where ultimate power—symbolized by the phallus—now resides. In some accounts, the exchange of women establishes masculinity and thus an individual's sovereign power, but even then, there is the nagging question of the relationship of the brothers to each other and to the father's law, which is taken to be the prohibition of incest that is at the very origin of society. All the brothers are presumed to be autonomous individuals, but what is the relationship between individual sovereignty and political power? What symbolically confirms political power? The end of monarchical rule brought with it a dispersed concept of sovereignty, but as an abstraction embodied in other abstractions (the individual, the people, the nation, its representatives). Although there would be many attempts to equate the phallus with the penis and so political power with masculinity, the fit was not as persuasive as when a single ruler wielded all the power. Indeed, the penis might be seen as a poor substitute for the large, central, and singular authority of the king. In any event, making the literal case for the penis as phallus has required continuous effort, the invention and reinvention of explanations. And it has not solved the matter of competition among the brothers. Can one of them ultimately take the father's place and so be exempt from, or above, the law? If so, which one? What are the signs of his exceptionalism? The search for answers to these questions plays out in the writing of constitutions, in the structure of political parties, in competition for office, in debates about the access of women to politics, and in varieties of political conflict, some of which have shaken the very foundations of the French nation-state.[31]

If, under the monarchy, seduction—representing more generally amorous relations between the sexes, the enactment of sexual difference—was a game for the politically impotent, in the democratic republic, seduction becomes one of the ways of asserting political power. It is a game in which the lines between the psychic and the political are blurred, and sexual difference is the key to both. Of course, even under absolutism, the phallus was a symbol whose psychic implementation was not bounded by real bodies or real-world politics, but the fact that it had a concrete referent arguably made a difference in the relationship between the realms of the psychic and the political.[32] Without the king, the phallus has no referent; its possession is up for grabs. No longer a signifier of a power that can be located in the occupant of the throne, the phallus is instead, in Lacan's terms, the signifier of desire instituted by lack. It is that which is constantly sought after but never possessed; in consequence, the operations of desire are driven by anxiety even if they give rise to temporary pleasures.

According to Lacan, sexuated subjects are constituted in relation to the phallus; these are psychic positionings, not biologically conferred identities, although it is sometimes difficult to entirely eliminate biological references when trying to explain these psychic positionings.[33] Lack means castration—not in the literal sense, but as alienation or separation, the loss of that sense of wholeness that marks an infant's imaginary connection to its mother, or of that imagined full presence implied by the idea of an autonomous individual. Psychoanalytic theory posits the phallus as the contradiction (in Žižek's terms, the "obscene underside") of republican political theory's concept of the autonomous individual.[34] In the place of self-willed, rational actors, there are subjects seeking to restore their imagined lost wholeness through their interactions with one another. The quest takes different forms, establishing subjects in dissymmetrical positions, either masculine or feminine. The masculine position seeks in its love objects a replacement for the phantasmatic lost mother. The desire of the Other(s) for him serves temporarily to assuage his loss, to seemingly overcome the paternal prohibition of incest, which is the origin of separation. The fantasy this enables is at least the appearance or illusion of possession of the phallus—in its traditional symbolic representation, as full presence and thus power. The feminine position both is defined in relation to the masculine and exceeds it. Access to the phallus (desire) is achieved, phantasmatically, in a relationship with a man (a relationship in which her desire serves his), but Lacan adds that women can also be an Other to themselves, thus escaping full enclosure in the phallic economy.[35]

Seduction from a Lacanian perspective, then, would be symptomatic of this phallic system—an economy in which the operations of desire are restless and incessant, and in which sexual difference is produced through inherently unstable psychic processes. In some ways, there is an analogy here to democratic political processes, but only an analogy. These democratic processes can be seen to be driven by desire, usually articulated as group interests; by contests for a power that has no settled referent, except the institutions—such as parliaments, presidents, and courts—in which the abstraction that is power is said to reside; and by dissymmetries in the positioning of citizens, the participants in the system, which are the outcome of previous struggles and long histories.

If this were the argument of aristocratic republicans, it might be persuasive, tempting us to provide genealogies of seduction over the *longue durée* of French history. But, as we shall see, theirs is another approach entirely, one that seeks to eliminate both the psychic anxieties of sexual difference and the inevitable tensions of democracy.

A Particular Form of Equality

For Ozouf and her colleagues, seduction sheds new light on the meaning of inequality. It is a system of balance in which the so-called natural differences of the sexes find a certain equilibrium. These differences ultimately refer to biology; there is none of the Lacanian psychic uncertainty or instability in the assumption of sexual identity. There are men and women, and there is a natural attraction between them, in which each has a different role to play. In fact, women are the civilizing force, curbing men's innate brutality. From this women derive their influence, a compensation for their lack of power. Habib writes that gallantry is "fundamentally inegalitarian. The point of departure of the relationship is the advantage that woman has over man, of being at the center of his desires. It's only a relative advantage: it's the force of masculine desire that establishes feminine power. The power is unequal; not all women profit from it. Moreover, it is transitory: one cannot hope to enjoy it all of one's life."[36] Women's role, she continues, is to "reassure" men that they will not be "gravely injured (*gravement lésés*) in the game of love. That was the major function of feminine virtue: it guaranteed to men—as much as possible—that respect for [of?] women was not a pure loss."[37] "As much as possible" at once acknowledges and dismisses the Lacanian version in which there is no remedy, no ultimate protection from the grave injury that is castration. For Habib, seduction is not the symptom but the resolution of the problem.

The arguments of the aristocratic republicans gesture to the noble tradition in which no one, it seemed, questioned their sexual identities. In which, as Habib puts it, there was "minimal agreement on the fact that something 'feminine' existed."[38] Modernity, in the form of feminists and homosexual militants, we are told, has compromised that tradition by claiming that individuals can decide on their own identities. Habib refers to "the grave disturbance (*ébranlement*) of sexual identities" and to "*la perplexité sexuelle*" that are the consequence of "a society of individuals." The conversion of feminine delicacy into claims for legal equality, talk of rights instead of the gentle murmurings of love, have led to a "brutalization of mores." She writes: "What is lost in the new arrangement is the refinement of amorous expression. We have lost the secret of it"[39]—and with it, women's ability to tame men's natural aggressiveness by totally submitting to their desire. The myth of seduction posits a time before sexual difference became a problem, and it suggests that there is still something in French national identity that escapes its difficulties. Gallantry, seduction's hallmark, rested on supposedly stable sexual identities whose inequalities were never protested; indeed, accepting inequality and working within its limits was the key to the pleasure that awaited the players in the game of seduction.

Inequality is the key to the importance of seduction for the ideology of aristocratic republicanism. Inequality is what Raynaud meant by "a particular form of equality." It is an inequality that he, Ozouf, and the others at once naturalize and eroticize. The difference between the sexes allows them to do both. If difference is undeniable, the point is to accept it. In any case, its inequities are superficial. Here is Ozouf, reviewing Habib: "The destiny of the two sexes is not symmetrical . . . love is never the triumph of the ego; to love someone is to wish for his well-being, even if it means subsuming one's personal ends; . . . this kind of attachment is not servitude. . . . There is, therefore, loving consent (*un consentement amoureux*), the fruit of natural attraction."[40]

Here, recognition for women is achieved through submission to the needs and will of one's superior, always a man. Seduction, which in more conventional usage denotes submission achieved by force or trickery, is now redefined as "loving consent."

Consent is important because it demonstrates the triumph of the rule of civility over the rule of law. Seduction is preferable to marriage not only because it emphasizes pleasure, but also because it involves no contract, no legal obligation. The bonds are established not for material considerations, but by passionate attraction. That is why attempts to legislate against sexual harassment are absurd. The police can never accomplish what only women can do: "civilize masculine desire."[41] Habib cites Montesquieu on the importance of manners: "Everything rests on this opposition between manners and laws; happy is the moderate legislator in a country where manners have taken the place of laws."[42] Citing this same quotation, Ozouf goes on to argue that it is precisely the superior importance of manners that has enabled Frenchwomen over the ages to understand "the inanity of juridical and political equality" when compared to the influence and pleasure they derive from their part in the game of seduction.[43] Habib notes that modern feminism's quest for recognition as "individuals equal in rights" destroys the very possibility for a loving relationship, which rests not on reason, but on passion and the inequality of woman and man—an inequality that, because it follows from the nature of things, nonetheless has its compensations.[44]

The endorsement of seduction as a form of loving consent, as an expression of art rather than law, is intended as a repudiation of feminists, often conflated with lesbians, who consider love to be a mask for male domination. Ozouf worries that feminism is the new Marxism. If for Marxism the final conflict was to lead to the end of class struggle and the leveling triumph of the proletariat, with feminism the outcome will be even more terrible: "the negation of the differences between the sexes." The negation takes two forms: the suppression of all visible evidence of difference and the radical repudiation of "natural attraction" by militant homosexuals. Homosexuality is depicted not as a plausible psychic position, but as an exclusively political project—a false utopia, "a dazzling promise"; for lesbians, the chimera of "an island rich in perfect equality" offering "an absolutely novel" "*jouis-*

sance féminine"—driven by the quest for an alternative to "the alliance of sex and power" that critics have mistakenly attributed to heterosexual coupling.[45] Habib notes that during her years in the feminist movements of the 1970s, "lesbians always struck me as blind elephants. They were in the shop, but they did not see the porcelain."[46]

Despite these disturbing deviations, the aristocratic republicans believe that France—marked, as a nation, by certain gendered characteristics—has been resistant to the siren call of feminism. For Raynaud, this is evident in a variety of indicators—the relative weakness or "humaneness" of French feminist culture; the absence in universities of women's studies programs "devoted to rereading the entire history of Western civilization from women's point of view"; the reluctance of female scholars to denounce canonical philosophy or literature as evidence of male domination; the historic willingness of Frenchwomen to accept the "delay" in access to suffrage—all of which indicate women's satisfaction with their destiny.[47] If scant evidence is offered to support these claims (for example, not all Frenchwomen willingly accepted the delay in access to suffrage; some protested it loudly) and if they might be explained in other ways (for example, by the control that educational hierarchies exercise over university curricula), that is of no concern to Raynaud.

It is a less tangible factor—the "spirit" of things—that really matters. Raynaud gives some examples:

> On the side of seduction, there has never been this massive boycott of the miniskirt by young Frenchwomen (as there was in the United States several months ago), we can see, on the contrary, an intentional emphasis on a sexy fashion aesthetic (that is not necessarily sexist); on the side of the family, even if there is commitment to equality, there is also a clearer distinction than elsewhere between the mother and the father; in the same spirit, we note that, when all tendencies are taken into account, French psychoanalysis is more comfortably loyal to the "phallocentric" aspects of Freud's thought.[48]

The disclaimers (garments are sexy but not sexist; families seek equality, but there are clear distinctions between mothers and fathers) attempt to disguise the conservatism of this vision, but it is clear that French culture remains "loyal" to the organization of sexuality around the phallus—by which Raynaud does not mean Lacan's signifier of desire, but the privileging of men.

The theory of seduction that these writers put forth dispenses with the uncertainty Lacan attributes to the phallus, insisting instead that in the game of love (and, as we shall see, in the game of politics as well) there is no question about where power lies. The appeal of aristocratic seduction in the age of absolutism lies precisely in the unequivocal and unchallenged position of the king. The possession of the phallus is never in doubt. In a move that reveals their mistaken reading of the past, these writers equate the king's power with male power in general. This may be where their story becomes myth, eliminating the troubling impotence of the nobility's game, opting instead for a more harmonious representation of history, and, at the same time, insisting that—in politics, as in sex—there is a real referent for the phallus.

Concern about the effects of feminism on men is evident in much of the writing on seduction, and it is often linked to rejection of an explicitly American feminism, which provides an ultraradical counterpoint to milder French forms. (Here is one of the ways of establishing a unique national identity, as a contrast to a reviled Other.) One example among many—Ozouf and Raynaud also attack American feminism as a kind of sexual Stalinism, and Habib attributes a crisis over the values of femininity to the publication of Simone de Beauvoir's *Second Sex*[49]—is a 1997 review by Jacques Julliard, editor of *Le Nouvel Observateur*, of an American book, one of those ephemeral publications that commentators rush to treat as the key to an entire society. The book was called *The Rules*, and it offered advice to women trying to snag a husband. Julliard objected to the reduction of the game of love to a set of written rules and to the power the book seemed to assign to women, though he found the approach typical of the long history of the United States: "The nightmare, par excellence, on the other side of the Atlantic . . . today, as yesterday, is love. To eliminate it, they have tried everything. First, repression, that is to say Puritanism. Then, trivialization, that is to say liberalized practices with their parade of scientific surveys and sexual gossip. Lastly, the final solution, that is to say American-style feminism."[50] He had witnessed the effects of this feminism, he reported, during a visit to a New England college campus: "I can assure you that the unfortunate boys who ventured into enemy territory had a cowering look—while the girls could talk about only one thing. Moreover, in order to escape the alleged lust of these males, the women had managed to hide their secondary sexual characteristics so well that it felt like Mao's China, and not the heart of Massachusetts."[51] So powerful a disincentive was the effect of this indifferentiation, Julliard commented, that "the sexual assaults these women feared" wouldn't be "so much criminal as heroic." He went on to lament the plight of American men, "those who suffer most": "Caught between the feminist party that wants to castrate him and the matrimonial party that dreams of caging him, the American male has limited chances of survival. Thus he [compensates]: he makes war and dreams of dominating the planet. For those of you preoccupied with American imperialism, it's useless to talk to their diplomats; better to whisper sweet nothings to their women."[52]

Julliard mounts his attack on American feminism as an implicit contrast favoring France, which he represents as the nation that isn't afraid of sex, knows how to play the game of seduction ("whisper sweet nothings"), and loves to love. Feminists bear the brunt of his attack. In his view, as in Ozouf's, legislating sexual relations results in castration. For Julliard, whether feminists insist that there are no differences between men and women or withdraw into an exclusive lesbianism, the effect is the same. So he issues an implicit warning to Frenchwomen by suggesting that generalized male violence is a reasonable response to feminism, and that rape is a "heroic" corrective to sexual indifferentiation. Habib offers another version of this idea when she insists that it is women who must tame male propensities to violence: "Because of their physiology, men have the means to associate, even to confound, aggression and *jouissance* . . . the dissociation of the two requires culture and artifice. It's a question of leading [men] to renounce predatory sexual pleasure, not by means of repression, but by persuasion. . . . The development of this kind of argument is the task of every woman."[53] After all, she adds, in a swipe at de Beauvoir, "one is not born gallant, one becomes it," and it is in "making herself loved that a woman succeeds in polishing a man."[54] Frenchwomen's patriotic duty, it would seem, is to stay away from feminism and thus spare their men the sufferings experienced by those across the Atlantic.

Julliard's repeated references to America as *l'outre Atlantique* secures the connection between sexual practices and national identity. The global political economy—which seems, among other things, to be reducing the salience of national boundaries—is driven, Julliard suggests, by emasculated Americans. The disappearance of clear lines of sexual difference serves both as a figure of this global homogenization and as a comment on its unnatural effects. The causality is reciprocal: sexual frustration drives American men to conquer the world, while their actions reproduce in the political and economic fields the pathology of the psychosexual realm.

Happily, these writers tell us, France has avoided American pathology in both the political and the sexual realm. Ozouf thinks that the men of the French Revolution may have implemented a stronger form of sexual segregation than existed during the ancien régime because they intuitively feared that the leveling effects of their radical democracy would lead to "a world without distinctions . . . an inhuman, gray abstraction"[55]—the world of Mao's China evoked by Julliard. Ozouf continues: "The praise of feminine difference protects democracy from itself."[56] The insistence on maintaining the boundaries of sexual difference, she says, kept the pattern of aristocratic seduction alive, even as the monarchy gave way to a succession of republics and the bourgeoisie eclipsed the nobility. And this, in turn, not only preserved the erotic side of life but offered a model for the subordination of all differences. Habib says that the legacy of absolutism made gallantry a compensation for subordination: "The society of Louis XIV was an ordered society, extremely hierarchical, from superior to inferior. . . . Gallantry was one of the variations on the art of accommodating to subordination."[57]

Ozouf offers seduction as a model for a politics in which there are no conflicts of power—the nation as an imagined affective community: "The threat posed by the real differences spread over French territory was easily vanquished only because of the deeply rooted emotional certainty of sharing an essence common to all the French. . . . At the same time, everyone could cultivate local differences, feeling their charm and their value, expressing them coquettishly or even with great pride, but without a spirit of dissent; differences without anxiety or aggression, contained within an abstract unity, and agreeing in advance to be subordinate to it."[58]

The harmony of the past ("differences without anxiety or aggression") is meant to correct the present's emphasis on conflicts of power and discrimination between men and women and, beyond that, among social groups. Instead of the intractability of power, with its spirit of dissent, we are offered the charms of seduction. The aim is to counter the claims of contemporary activists by proclaiming the existence of *"un génie national"* with deep historical roots that these dissidents have misunderstood or want to destroy. Whether the dissidents are feminists demanding equal access to politics (*parité*), gay activists seeking the right to form families (through marriage, adoption, and access to reproductive technologies), or Muslims defending the hijab as a legitimate form of women's religious observance, they are said to be challenging the very existence of the national community.

Aristocratic republicanism, with sexual difference at its core, insists on subordinating particular differences to an abstract unity and is meant to serve the strategic purpose of separating "true" French from "foreign" elements, connecting the proper heirs to their history. It is not surprising that the connection between seduction (an asymmetrical relationship between two different subjects) and national unity (the submersion of all differences into an abstract single identity) is first located in the monarchy of Louis XIV. While the nobility played erotic games of simulated power, the king established himself as the embodiment of the nation. But this idea of the connection between seduction and national unity also takes republican political theory into account. Historically, that theory has identified the universal with the masculine, the particular with the feminine. In effect, Habib, Ozouf, and the others restate this theory by repeatedly emphasizing the need for female subjects (who are particular and different) to subordinate themselves to male subjects (the embodiment of the universal), willingly and with great affection. The merger of the two—aristocracy and republic—is achieved by identifying power (the phallus) with masculinity. The ambiguities of democracy are averted when men (or those clearly dominant—that is, native, white French people) are, in effect, made king.

The importance, then, of the theory of seduction is that it offers an affective model with deep historical roots for politics: "an essence common to all the French." The heterosexual couple embodies difference not as a field of force, but as a shifting play of contrasting and complementary elements (delightful to experience and to behold). Within the couple, the natural subordination of women to men replicates the accommodation that any social difference must make in the interests of national harmony. If force is introduced into the relationship, seduction loses its allure and becomes a violent struggle; militant homosexuality—in its refusal of difference—is the abhorrent consequence of the distortion of the natural ties of heterosexual erotics. By extension, any group that protests its different treatment, that enters the political arena claiming an equality it has been denied, is a threat to national integrity. Homophobia thus functions both to ensure the heterosexual couple's iconic function and to guard against the leveling effects of democracy. Tellingly, the very conflicts that democracy was designed to mediate become, in this conservative nationalist vision, threats to the social fabric itself.

The Politics of the Veil

The French theory of seduction has been articulated to counter the claims of various dissident groups in French society. Ozouf and Julliard take feminism as their primary target. So does Habib, but she adds Muslims to the list of those who are at odds with the French way of life. French aversion to head scarves, she suggests, has had less to do with racism or the persistence of Jacobin secularism than with "an implicit norm about the relations between the sexes—the ascendancy of feminine beauty and the fidelity of men."[59] Citing the veil as a repudiation of women's sexuality, Habib compares it to the adoration women received at court, where they mixed freely with men. It was their appearance, so artfully crafted to please and attract, that gave them entry to the game of seduction. Visibility was vital to the very meaning of femininity, however artificial the improvements of clothing, coiffure, and powder. And the tradition of gallantry depended not only on women's visibility but on "pleasure and joy in being visible. . . . Wearing the veil indicates chastity and that signified the interruption, and even the impossibility, of the gains of gallantry. There is no possible conciliation."[60] In her review of Habib's book, Ozouf made the point more strongly. The aristocratic heritage persisted stubbornly, she suggested, "in the natural inclination of women not to separate love and sexuality, in their distaste for separation, in their dream to make their commitments long-term."[61] (This last point is one of the many times a contradiction arises between seduction as a transitory game and the desire for permanence, at least on the part of women.) To the extent that the game of seduction was an essential French trait, Muslims' failure to play it meant they could never be fully French.

Habib's explanation of French objections to the veil makes sense; they are the objections of an "open society" to a "closed one," a recognition of differences of cultural style.[62] I have made a similar argument about the underlying motive for the head scarf ban in my book on the issue.[63] What makes my argument different from Habib's, however, is that she insists that French traditions are more natural, or at least superior, in their handling of the differences between the sexes, and also that the closed nature of Muslim society disqualifies Muslims from membership in the nation. But there is more. In her eyes, Muslims pose a threat to the continuity of the old tradition of seduction. Their practices "interrupt" the game, blocking "the circulation of *coquetterie* and *hommage*," offering another set of rules for the relations of the sexes—strict separation. The veil "flouts an implicit norm of what ought to be the relations between the sexes—the ascendance of feminine beauty and masculine allegiance to it." And, by condemning "that which has been elaborated through the centuries as a form of coexistence between the sexes," Muslims threaten its endurance.[64]

In her book, Ozouf cites Montesquieu's fictional report on the reaction of two Persians visiting France in the early eighteenth century—an example of early Orientalism that she takes to be a reflection of the real differences between East and West: "Here, a style of equality between the sexes, and of liberty. No veils, no bars, no eunuchs. . . . Behind the appearance of equality, the reality of women's supremacy."[65] The Persians take the absence of patriarchal control, "the power to keep watch over and punish," to be disastrous for a well-regulated family, but Ozouf equates sharp lines of segregation with male domination in ways that powerfully echo the contemporary discussion of Muslim veils. For her, *mixité*—the mixing of the sexes in public space—means greater freedom on both sides, but particularly for women. As she describes what Montesquieu imagines the Persians saw in Paris, she cannot restrain her delight: "Women with no inhibition prepare their toilette and their faces with the sole purpose of seducing; [they are] skillful at changing not only their costume, but their very bodies; [they are] out of their minds with luxuriousness, devoted to the game, breaking off to control the pace of conversation and to cut off the speech of men of science and intellect."[66] Erotic attraction gave women a certain superiority, even as they dedicated themselves to the delight of men; they might "cut off" men's speech, but there was no threat of castration here; no law could install this "particular form of equality."

By rooting contemporary French attitudes in an ancestral habit, Habib and Ozouf essentialize Frenchness and so write Muslims out of membership in the national community. Muslims are portrayed as strangers, an unnatural people with no rightful place in the history of this nation. The fact that, of course, they do have a rightful place in a long history of colonial and postcolonial experience is obscured by the invocation of the seductive ancestors. Muslims' demands for the recognition of their rightful place in the representation of the nation are disqualified because their attitudes and behaviors are too different to fit in. Their calls for an end to group discrimination also raise the issue of difference in a politically dangerous way, one taken to be consonant with the Islamic system of sex segregation. Rather than subordinate difference to the dominant way of doing things, these political actors take difference to be an organizing principle. And in politics they seek to use difference as a lever to alter the structures of power that marginalize or exclude them. For the seduction theorists, however, the game of politics, like that of aristocratic seduction, must be played as if such structures and power did not exist. Those who don't know the rules of the game are not considered viable players, in matters of politics as in matters of love. Thus the conclusion is that France is not denying Muslims' rights; rather, the Muslims—in their management of sexual difference and, by extension, of all human relationships—are disqualifying themselves as French.

The Seduction of the Sign

It might be said that the conservative nationalist intellectuals I have been discussing are themselves practicing the art of seduction in the terms that Jean Baudrillard used to describe it in 1979: "It is because the sign has been turned from its meaning or 'seduced' that the story itself is seductive. It is when signs are seduced that they become seductive."[67] In the literary tradition of aristocratic gentility, the intellectuals find a story that leaves out the messy details of betrayal, power, and exploitation, recasting hierarchies of dependence in terms of civility and gallantry. They refuse the challenges that have been posed to social prescriptions for sexual difference, conflating the normative with the natural, the natural with the cultural, and the cultural with the national. Rather than the restless and irrepressible movement of desire, seduction becomes a predictable expression of heterosexuality—the only kind of sexual relationship that is plausible and satisfying.

It is, first of all, sexual difference that is seduced in the story these intellectuals tell. As if to stabilize the inherently contradictory union that is aristocratic republicanism, they present the heterosexual relationship as natural and unproblematic, the only possible resolution to those primal and unresolved questions about the links between anatomy, sexuality, and identity. The tensions and conflicts that attend relations between the sexes are attributed to contemporary troublemakers—such as feminists and homosexuals—who are out of touch with what history supposedly teaches us are natural human inclinations. These inclinations extend from sex to politics; the hierarchy of the couple becomes a model for social organization.

In the process, equality is also seduced, turned from its historical meaning in the French Revolution and the current French Constitution to represent something else entirely—a game of appearances that rests on illusion, with no end but mutual pleasure. Equality is not to be measured by the distribution of jobs, wages, or legal rights, but by another standard entirely—one that has to do with erotic exchanges between the sexes, with the rules of the game of seduction.

In this version of equality, the nationalist intellectuals have fashioned a *trompe l'oeil*, in which the equality of republican theory is exemplified by aristocratic erotic games marked by asymmetry between partners, and in which politics are embodied by a (necessarily French) couple. The trick of these examples, of course, is to demonstrate that inequalities are, if not actually equality, then a complementarity of differences always subordinate to the unity of the nation. In this way, these nationalists have sought to distract their readers from the difficulties that republicans are having in figuring out how to reconcile their commitment to universalism with the problem of long-standing inequities (of wages, resources, social and political access, and recognition) in the treatment of groups (women, Muslims, homosexuals, and others) marked by their difference from the universal (masculine) individual. If, in the theory of seduction, man and woman stand for the universal and the particular, and if nature requires her submission to his desire—indeed, rewards her with love for that willing submission—then the message to France's others is clear: play the game with loving consent, and you will reap rewards appropriate to your status. The style of engagement—flirtatiousness, gallantry, civility—matters too. It marks you not only as a legitimate player in the game, but as deeply and incontestably French.

Epilogue

A Feminist Theory Archive

IN AN ESSAY SHE WROTE IN 2003, which reviewed feminist psychoanalytic literary criticism, Elizabeth Weed talked of the energy
and excitement, the sexual sparkle and the sheer pleasure—one might
even say the jouissance—one felt when encountering feminist writing
in the 1970s and 1980s. Citing Janet Malcolm's 1987 *New Yorker* review
of *In Dora's Case: Freud, Hysteria, Feminism*, Weed notes Malcolm's
particular appreciation of the feminist writings in that collection.[1] It
is their emancipated tone, the transferential quality of their criticism
(they fantasize wildly and irreverently about the master theorists)
that delights Malcolm—and Weed, who notes: "One might even argue that it was the unabashedly transferential nature of early feminist
criticism more than its political character that opponents found dis-
concerting. At least until Harold Bloom's "Anxiety of Influence," even
literary criticism, probably the least detached of the critical disciplines, could perform its work at a reassuring remove. Academic
feminism changed that. This is not to say that all feminist criticism of
the seventies through the late eighties shone forth with an irresistible,
gleeful energy. But there was a general excitement in that early work."[2]

It is an excitement Weed finds lacking in more recent writing, although she notes that there is much to be admired and learned from
the newer focus on once-neglected questions of race, ethnicity, sexuality, and discrimination. As she describes it, the shift from defiant
engagement with fathers to exegeses informed by theories of trauma
and melancholia involves a very different affect, another tone entirely,
and a changed relation to politics. Weed does not write out of nostalgia for a lost world, but there is surely a bit of regret in her essay, even
as it appreciates a new generation of feminist literary scholarship.

I think some of that regret became the inspiration for the Feminist
Theory Papers, an archival collection that Weed launched at Brown
University's John Hay Library. The archive was not conceived of as a
monument either to dead feminists (although a need to find a home
for the papers of the literary scholar Naomi Schor was an immediate
factor in its creation) or to an expired social and political movement.
It was not a compensatory gesture meant to prove that women, too,
deserved a place in the annals of philosophical thought. Nor was it an
attempt to collect the documentation for an authoritative and sys-
tematized version of feminist theory in the way that the earliest
archives were used to authorize the rule of monarchs and nations.
Memory surely was at issue—any archive is a prompt to memory—
but there was no aim to direct or control it for some clearly defined
end. The idea was not to immortalize a certain kind of theorist from a
certain historical period as the embodiment of a one true feminism.
Rather, the point was to insist, in the face of the current backlash
against feminism and theory, that these were not ephemeral moments
but events, in Foucault's sense of the word—major discursive shifts
with far-reaching and continuing ramifications.

Foucault refers to the archive as "the set of discourses actually
pronounced," the set that determines what counts as knowledge in a
particular period.[3] There is no homogeneity in Foucault's archive, but
a "density of discursive practices, systems that establish statements as
events (with their own conditions and domain of appearance) and
things (with their own possibility and field of use)."[4] The feminist
theory gathered in this archive is part of a set of discourses, evidence
that there are contests about what counts as knowledge, that knowledge is no sure or commonly agreed upon thing, even within what

might be called a discursive or cultural "system." Here is Foucault again: "Far from being that which unifies everything that has been said in the great confused murmur of a discourse, far from being only that which ensures that we exist in the midst of preserved discourse, [the archive] is that which differentiates discourses in their multiple existence and specifies them in their own duration."[5] From this perspective, the decision to collect and house the papers of a generation and more of feminist scholars is an effort to continue the critical work they (we) engage in by attributing to it value as history. I don't mean history in the sense of something dead and gone, but rather something worth holding onto—a living heritage, if you will, an enduring legacy. This archive is a living reminder, a rebuke to currently fashionable "post" thinking on questions of theory and feminism. It is a post-post institution. It marks not the exhaustion or the death of feminist theory, but its continuing vitality.

When she conceived the plan for the archive, Weed (having read Derrida's *Archive Fever*),[6] wondered if there might be a contradiction at its core between the conservative tendency of any archive and the avowed commitment to revolution of the contributors to this one. What did it mean to contain corrosive critique in acid-free boxes, to subject it to a host of technological operations (classifying, cataloging, digitizing) and to confine it in categories suitable for an index (however sympathetically devised)? Would critique survive its imprisonment, or would it become domesticated, inevitably succumbing to history's disciplinary requirements? And even if these were not objectionable practices, did an attempt to preserve the critical thinking of another era undermine the very purpose of critique, which was to deconstruct the legacies of the past in order to open new ways for thinking the future? Would putting these papers in an archive impose the weight of the past, the burden of tradition, on the possibilities for new thought? Would it confirm the idea that origins—of movements, ideas, and events—can really be found? Was it possible that what was once lively critique would become stultifying orthodoxy? These are troubling questions when posed abstractly, and I suggest that they could be posed only by philosophers and others who haven't spent much time in archives. Historians know there is a different reality, albeit not free of its own difficulties.

The archive that historians work in is not a prison with numbered, locked cells or, for that matter, a cemetery, where rows of tombstones inscribed with names and dates convey a sense of finality and closure. The historian's archive is not a mournful place, but one where the living continue to find life. Writing in the *New Yorker*, Jill Lepore likened a Cryonics Institute (a place where the dead are frozen, awaiting their ultimate resurrection) to an archive: "a place where people deposit their papers—the contents of their heads—when they're dead, so that someone, some future historian, can find them and bring them back to life."[7] The conceit of cheating death is widespread among historians. Or perhaps it is better to say that historians make death a minor episode, something that is transitory rather than final. Metaphors abound: there are shadows materialized by light; ghosts given embodiment; corpses exhumed for a second life. Whispers are heard from "the souls who had suffered so long ago and who were smothered now in the past."[8] Jules Michelet, the nineteenth-century French historian, consummately lyrical, is wonderful to listen to on this. "As I breathed their dust," he writes of his contact with the dead in old papers and leather-bound parchments, "I saw them rise up. They rose from the sepulchre . . . as in the Last Judgment of Michelangelo or in the Dance of Death. This frenzied dance . . . I have tried to reproduce in [my] work."[9] It's tempting here to think of these dancers experiencing *la petite mort*—the little death—which in French is synonymous with jouissance. The orgiastic frenzy of the dancers evokes the image, as does Michelet's own obvious pleasure in recounting the story.

Carolyn Steedman has written a book called *Dust*, a social historian's reply to Derrida's philosophical musings on the archive. (Among other things, she insists—playing with the reputation of the social historian for reading literally—that if there is archive fever, it may have to do with the actual inhalation of dust and with traces of anthrax clinging to the sheepskin bindings one touches there. This is also, of course, a metaphor for the persistence of the past, its ability to infect those who come into contact with it.) In the book, Steedman stresses the importance of randomness and accident, even in the most carefully constructed archives, those whose origins lie with the rationalizing impulses of state power: "The Archive is made from selected and consciously chosen documentation from the past and also from the mad fragmentations that no one intended to preserve and that just ended up there."[10] Mad fragmentations sit waiting in the interstices of assigned categories to engage the imagination of the lonely researcher who, these days, is not usually looking for origins, but rather documentation for an interpretation she wants to advance. I should add that researchers are rarely confined by the formal classifying rubrics; they routinely refuse to be limited by them. Indeed, part of the fun of archival research is guessing what might be found in a box of papers whose label is seemingly irrelevant to the inquiry at hand. Historians, even the most conventional, know that what they are looking for may not be what some archivist thought it was.

The pursuit of knowledge in the archive is a highly individualized task, but it's not lonely. The researcher surrounds herself with the whispering souls she conjures from the material she reads. If she's a good reader, she listens, too, for silences and omissions. She ponders the apparent order of thoughts and texts. Michel de Certeau, referring to Foucault, says that "to think . . . is to pass through: it is to question that order, to marvel that it exists, to wonder what made it possible, to seek, in passing over its landscape, traces of the movement that formed it, to discover in these histories supposedly laid to rest, 'how and to what extent it would be possible to think otherwise.' "[11] It is the historian's engagement with what she finds there that makes the archive a dynamic, social place, one in which the objects of her desire also have something of a life of their own.

The challenge, of course, for all but the most naive empiricists, is that the texts don't speak for themselves; the whispers are heard only through a process of translation, and the very words—spoken or written—carry different meanings in each of their iterations. The dead don't come back to life as they were, but as we represent them. Michelet thought he was exhuming *le peuple* and so revealing their deepest desire, but his—as any history—was a work of projection and interpretation.[12] Barthes adds that it was also a work of incorporation —Michelet, he wrote, "actually ate history," as Christians eat the blood and body of their savior, and in this way both approach and transcend death.[13] Again, I would offer la petite mort as the apposite term—the momentary conjunction of the psychic drives of death and life. Steedman, however, suggests that the "sedentary, airless, and fevered scholarly life spent in close proximity to leather bound books and documents" means that infection by anthrax actually made Michelet ill.[14]

The problem of the archive, for me, is not that it systematizes and preserves; it's the reading practices to which the contents are subjected. The question of representation, not unique by any means to archival holdings, at once saves us from the threat of stagnation and threatens the integrity of what is there. I would like to protect the past from its appropriation by the wrong kind of people: those who read literally, who are deaf to language's resonances, who recuperate critical concepts for normative uses, and who seek to confirm their identities by locating ancestors who are just like them. My greatest fears about my own papers are that they'll be used to prove some ideologically driven point that has never been my own, that the things I value most will be trivialized, and that the trivial will assume an undeserved importance. I'd rather be dead than misread. For that reason, I've considered eliminating from the papers I give to Brown the items that I think are most susceptible to misreading. It's because I know history is about representation that I want to control my own.

But I also understand the futility of trying to exercise that control. It's impossible to foresee what among those papers will lend themselves to misuse. More important, my impulse for control contradicts my commitment to critique. When I think about the uses to which my artifacts could be put, I become the worst kind of objective historian, insisting on the transparent meaning of what's there. My work has, after all, achieved a certain legitimacy in the world of feminist theory in which I travel; it's a legitimacy I want preserved on my terms. Yet the theory it stands for endorses the notions that no thinking is immune from critique, that the pursuit of knowledge is an unending and often discontinuous process, that futures cannot be bound to or by the past.

Derrida understood this dilemma as he sketched plans for the Collège de Philosophie in the early 1980s:

> The most ruthless critique, the implacable analysis of a power of legitimation is always produced in the name of a system of legitimation. . . . We already know that the interest in research not currently legitimated will only find its way if, following trajectories ignored by or unknown to any

established institutional power, this new research is *already underway and promises a new legitimacy* until one day, once again . . . and so on. We also know—and who wouldn't want it?—that if the Collège is created with the resources it requires and, above all, if its vitality and richness are one day what we foresee, then it will become in its turn a legitimating instance that will have obligated many other instances to reckon with it. It is this situation that must be continuously analyzed, today and tomorrow, to avoid exempting the Collège from its own analytic work.[15]

Unlike an educational institution, which has the task of certifying its graduates, an archive has no responsibility for the uses made of it. Of course, archivists try to impose order on the mass of papers they must process, and they set standards for selection, and thus for inclusion and exclusion. But they can't really rein in the imaginations of the researchers sitting there, inhaling the dust. It's not only the mad fragments that draw one's attention, the odd pieces that dispel the tedium of scholarly research. It's also the operations of our psyches— always incompletely disciplined—that attach us to substitutes for the lost objects of our childhood, or draw us to outbursts of passion in forms we don't understand, or lead us to judgments that aren't always rationally defensible.[16] How can we account for our attraction to (or repulsion from) specific events, philosophies, figures, or, for that matter, figures of speech? I'm not calling for psychoanalytic testing as a prerequisite for users of archives. The point is that the archive is a provocation; its contents offer an endless resource for thinking and rethinking. Steedman puts it this way: "The Archive, then, is something that, through the cultural activity of History, can become Memory's potential space, one of the few realms of the modern imagination where a hard-won and carefully constructed place, can return to boundless, limitless space."[17] I like the way she juxtaposes place—a definable physical location (the John Hay Library, in the case of the Feminist Theory Papers)—and space—the illimitable realm of imagination, where our past, present, and future selves and those of others intersect unpredictably. I'm not saying that anything goes. Of course there is discipline; inquiry cannot proceed without it. But it's the confrontation, the contrast of discourses—to go back to Foucault for a minute—that produces excitement and thus new knowledge. As he says, the archive "is that which differentiates discourses in their multiple existence and specifies them in their own duration."[18] I would add that the user of the archives is part of that discursive mix. The archive is a place that opens the space in which critique can flourish.

There's nothing contradictory about housing theory in an archive. What would we do without the papers of Kant, Hegel, Marx, the Frankfurt School, Simone de Beauvoir, and dozens of other practitioners of critique? We'd not only know less about how and why they thought as they did, but we'd be deprived of the practical details of the articulation of critique (whom they read and wrote to; how they qualified, expanded, or changed their ideas, and in what political, social, economic, and personal contexts). And we'd lack the resources by which to gain insight into the affective side of their thought processes. Most of all, though, we'd lose the stuff that imagination thrives on and by which it pleasures itself. Our own critical faculty gets off, not only on following their example, but on knowing more about them and then critiquing and exceeding what they've done.

We can't prevent the dullards from reading our papers, and they will surely represent us in ways we cannot abide. But the bet one makes in leaving behind the records of a life (or, for that matter, in writing a book) committed to critical thought is that some readers will be moved to think with us, albeit differently. If our own death is certain, we give the next generation of historians the occasion for la petite mort—the extraordinary pleasure that comes not only from exposure to brave and courageous ideas, transgressive acts, and bold and irreverent behavior, but also from the need to puzzle over these things in order to understand them in the difference of their historical moments. Will a new generation of scholars read us differently? Will they sense the same excitement that so moved Janet Malcolm and Elizabeth Weed? Will they experience the same pleasure or, indeed, any pleasure at all?

Jouissance is by definition transitory. In that way, it's like critique. And, like critique, it recurs (though never in the same way) if the circumstances are right. Archives—books too—can't contain or preserve jouissance, but they provide the materials for its recurrence. In the process it's not only the researchers who change, but the materials as well. The repository of papers then is anything but a dead-letter office; instead, it is the place and the space from which new ideas can issue forth without end.

Notes

Introduction

1. Harold T. Parker, "Review Essay: A Methodological Gem," *Journal of Urban History* 2, no. 3 (1976): 373–76.

2. It is now too late to thank him for his advice. Professor Parker died, at age ninety-four, in 2002.

3. Michel de Certeau, *The Writing of History*, trans. Tom Conley (New York: Columbia University Press, 1988), 288.

4. For my objections, see Joan Wallach Scott, "Gender: A Useful Category of Historical Analysis," *American Historical Review* 91, no. 5 (1986): 1053–75.

5. See Joan Wallach Scott, "Finding Critical History," in *Becoming Historians*, ed. James Banner and John Gillis (Chicago: University of Chicago Press, 2009), 26–53.

6. Certeau, *The Writing of History*, 343. Thanks to postcolonial history, the "law of place" is no longer taken for granted. See, for example, Dipesh Chakrabarty, *Provincializing Europe: Postcolonial Thought and Historical Difference* (Princeton: Princeton University Press, 2000); Andrew Zimmerman, *Alabama in Africa: Booker T. Washington, the German Empire and the Globalization of the New South* (Princeton: Princeton University Press, 2010); and Kathleen Wilson, *The Island Race: Englishness, Empire, and Gender in the Eighteenth Century* (London: Routledge, 2003).

7. Certeau, *The Writing of History*, 288.

8. Ibid., 291.

9. Ibid., 303.

10. I am aware of the arguments (from queer theorists and some feminist theorists) that caution against the use of "sexual difference" as a psychoanalytic, or indeed any analytic, tool because it seems to assume a fixed relationship between the physical body, gender, and sexuality that reproduces prevailing heterosexual norms. For example, Didier Eribon argues that psychoanalysis *tout court* is inherently homophobic. See his *Echapper à la psychanalyse* (Paris: Léo Scheer, 2005) and *Hérésies: Essais sur la théorie de la sexualité* (Paris: Fayard, 2003). Only if sexual difference is posited as having inherent and unalterable meaning is this a problem. My argument is that psychoanalysis in fact disputes the idea of any possible direct correlation between physical bodies and psychic identifications. It posits sexual difference as a dilemma that is unresolvable, hence open to all manner of variations in the way it is lived. The fact that the variations are at once infinite (fantasy enables this) and constrained (by normative regulation) opens our analyses to historicization of individuals and groups in their temporally bounded contexts.

11. For a historical overview, see Peter Burke, "Freud and Cultural History," *Psychoanalysis and History* 9, no. 1 (2007): 5–15; Peter Loewenberg, *Decoding the Past: The Psychohistorical Approach* (New York: Alfred Knopf, 1983), and *Fantasy and Reality in History* (New York: Oxford University Press, 1995); Frank Manuel, "The Use and Abuse of Psychoanalysis for History," *Daedalus* 100, no. 1 (1971): 187–213.

12. Gayle Rubin, "The Traffic in Women: Notes on the 'Political Economy' of Sex," in *Toward an Anthropology of Women*, ed. Rayna R. Reiter (New York: Monthly Review Press, 1975), 157–210.

13. Natalie Zemon Davis, " 'Women's History' in Transition: The European Case," *Feminist Studies* 3, no. 3–4 (1976): 90.

14. Parveen Adams and Elizabeth Cowie, eds., *The Woman in Question: m/f* (Cambridge: MIT Press, 1990); Judith Butler, *Gender Trouble: Feminism and the Subversion of Identity* (New York: Routledge, 1990); Donna J. Haraway, *Simians, Cyborgs, and Women: The Reinvention of Nature* (New York: Routledge, 1991).

15. Parveen Adams and Jeffrey Minson, "The 'Subject' of Feminism," in Adams and Cowie, *The Woman in Question*, 99.

16. Louis Althusser, "Ideology and Ideological State Apparatuses," in Louis Althusser, *Lenin and Philosophy, and Other Essays*, trans. Ben Brewster (New York: Monthly Review Press, 1972), 127–88.

17. Denise Riley, *"Am I That Name?" Feminism and the Category of "Women" in History* (London: Macmillan, 1988), 7.

18. Ibid.

19. Ibid., 5.

20. Ibid., 2.

21. Ibid., 104.

22. Ibid., 102.

23. See, for example, Tania Modleski, *Feminism without Women: Culture and Criticism in a Postfeminist Age* (New York: Routledge, 1991).

24. Riley, *"Am I That Name?,"* 7.

25. Ibid., 50.

26. Judith Butler, *Undoing Gender* (New York: Routledge, 2004), 186.

27. Joan Copjec, "Cutting Up," in *Between Feminism and Psychoanalysis*, ed. Teresa Brennan (New York: Routledge, 1989), 229. See also Joan Copjec, *Read My Desire: Lacan against the Historicists* (Cambridge: MIT Press, 1996).

28. Copjec, "Cutting Up," 238.

29. Ibid., 241–42.

30. Ibid., 238.

31. Certeau, *The Writing of History*, 303.

32. Sigmund Freud, "Constructions in Analysis," in *The Standard Edition of the Complete Psychological Works of Sigmund Freud*, trans. James Strachey et al. (London: The Hogarth Press, 1995 edition), XXIII: 259. All future references to Freud will be to this standard edition and marked "SE."

33. Ibid., 263.

34. Ibid., 268.

35. Jean Laplanche and Jean-Bertrand Pontalis, *The Language of Psycho-analysis*, trans. Donald Nicholson-Smith (New York: W. W. Norton, 1974), 89.

36. Copjec, "Cutting Up," 242.

37. Michel Foucault, *The Order of Things: An Archaeology of the Human Sciences* (New York: Vintage, 1994), 322.

38. Ibid., 330.

39. Ibid., 380.

40. Ibid., 373.

41. Ibid., 379.

42. Ibid., 374.

43. Ibid., 376.

44. Ibid., 394.

45. Ibid., 374.

46. Elizabeth Weed, "Gender and Sexual Difference in Joan W. Scott: From the 'Useful' to the 'Impossible,'" in *The Question of Gender: Engaging with Joan W. Scott's Critical Feminism*, ed. Judith Butler and Elizabeth Weed (Bloomington: Indiana University Press, 2012). There are, of course, scholars who insist that Foucault cannot be reconciled with psychoanalysis. For example, Eribon writes: "C'est Foucault ou la psychanalyse" (It's either Foucault or psychoanalysis; *Echapper à la psychanalyse*, 86). Others, however, offer readings that find greater sympathy for psychoanalysis in Foucault. See, for example, Charles Shepherdson, *Vital Signs: Nature, Culture, Psychoanalysis* (New York: Routledge, 2000); Suzanne Gearhart, "The Taming of Foucault: New Historicism, Psychoanalysis and the Subversion of Power," *New Literary History* 28, no. 3 (1997): 457–80, a "Reply to Stephen Greenblatt," *New Literary History* 28, no. 3 (1997): 483–85; Judith

Butler, *The Psychic Life of Power: Theories in Subjection* (Stanford: Stanford University Press, 1997).

47. Debra Keates, "Sexual Difference," in *Feminism and Psychoanalysis: A Critical Dictionary*, ed. Elizabeth Wright (Oxford: Basil Blackwell, 1992), 402–5.

48. Butler, *Undoing Gender*, 186.

49. Judith Butler, *Bodies That Matter: On the Discursive Limits of "Sex"* (New York: Routledge, 1993), 99.

50. Laplanche and Pontalis, *The Language of Psycho-analysis*, 440.

51. Elizabeth Weed, "Feminist Psychoanalytic Literary Criticism," in *The Cambridge Companion to Feminist Literary Theory*, ed. Ellen Rooney (Cambridge: Cambridge University Press, 2006), 262.

52. Joan Wallach Scott, *Only Paradoxes to Offer: French Feminists and the Rights of Man* (Cambridge: Harvard University Press, 1996), and *Parité: Sexual Equality and the Crisis of French Universalism* (Chicago: University of Chicago Press, 2005).

53. Weed, "Gender and Sexual Difference in Joan W. Scott." See also Bruce Fink, *The Lacanian Subject: Between Language and Jouissance* (Princeton: Princeton University Press, 1995), 104. It is this asymmetry of masculine and feminine positions that leads Lacan to conclude that "there is no such thing as a sexual relationship." I discuss this more fully in chapter 5.

54. Simone de Beauvoir, *The Second Sex*, trans. H. M. Parshley (New York: Random House, 1974).

55. See "Forum on Transnational Sexualities," *American Historical Review* 114, no. 5 (2009), 1250–353.

56. Slavoj Žižek, *The Plague of Fantasies* (London: Verso, 1997); Renata Salecl, *The Spoils of Freedom: Psychoanalysis and Feminism after the Fall of Socialism* (London: Routledge, 1994).

57. Jean Laplanche, *New Foundations for Psychoanalysis*, trans. David Macey (London: Basil Blackwell, 1989), 41–45.

58. François Duparc, "Secondary Revision," in *International Dictionary of Psychoanalysis*, 3 vols., ed. Alain de Mijolla, 3:1558–60 (Framington Hills, Mich.: Thomson Gale, 2005). See also François Duparc, *L'Image sur le divan* (Paris: L'Harmattan, 1995); Freud, "The Interpretation of Dreams," SE V: 488–508.

59. Thanks to Ben Kafka for this point (made in private conversation) and for directing me to Duparc.

60. Donald G. Mathews and Jane Sherron De Hart, *Sex, Gender, and the Politics of the ERA: A State and the Nation* (New York: Oxford University Press, 1990). See also Jean Walton, *Fair Sex, Savage Dreams: Race, Psychoanalysis, Sexual Difference* (Durham: Duke University Press, 2001).

61. We need more theorizing about the creation of collective fantasies and the use of individual fantasies for political or social ends. It would be useful, for example, to think about how secondary revision actually works in concrete

situations. For an attempt to think about fantasy along Lacanian lines, see Žižek, *The Plague of Fantasies.*

62. Certeau, *The Writing of History,* 303.

63. William L. Langer, "The Next Assignment," *American Historical Review* 63, no. 2 (1958): 284. Thanks to Brian Connolly for pointing me to Langer's speech.

64. Freud, "Creative Writers and Day-Dreaming," SE IX: 148.

65. Certeau, *The Writing of History,* 304.

1. Feminism's History

This chapter was originally written for presentation at a panel on "The Future of Feminist History" at the American Historical Association meeting in January 2003.

1. Lois Banner and Mary S. Hartman, eds., *Clio's Consciousness Raised: New Perspectives on the History of Women, Sex and Class in Women's History* (New York: Harper and Row, 1974).

2. Plato, *Phaedrus,* trans. R. Hackforth (Cambridge: Cambridge University Press, 1952), 57.

3. I am grateful to Froma Zeitlin for the references that provided this information.

4. The special issue was *differences* 9, no. 3 (1997). It was published, with additional essays, as Joan Wallach Scott, *Women's Studies on the Edge* (Durham: Duke University Press, 2009).

5. Anne Firor Scott, Sara M. Evans, Susan K. Cahn, and Elizabeth Faue, "Women's History in the New Millennium: A Conversation across Three Generations; Part I," *Journal of Women's History* 11, no. 1 (1999): 9–30, and "Women's History in the New Millennium: A Conversation across Three Generations; Part II," *Journal of Women's History* 11, no. 2 (1999): 199–220.

6. This is the case both domestically and internationally, evident most visibly in the work of the UN Committee on the Elimination of Discrimination against Women, or CEDAW. See Françoise Gaspard, "Les femmes dans les relations internationales," *Politique Étrangère* 3, no. 4 (2000): 731–41.

7. Jacques Derrida, "Women in the Beehive: A Seminar," in *Men in Feminism,* ed. Alice Jardine and Paul Smith (New York: Methuen, 1987), 190.

8. Bill Readings, *The University in Ruins* (Cambridge: Harvard University Press, 1996), 32.

9. Nancy Cott, *The Grounding of Modern Feminism* (New Haven: Yale University Press, 1987).

10. Plato, *Phaedrus,* 57.

11. Scott, Evans, Cahn, and Faue, "Women's History in the New Millennium: A Conversation across Three Generations; Part I," 9–30, and "Part II," 199–220.

12. Carroll Smith-Rosenberg, "The Female World of Love and Ritual: Relations between Women in Nineteenth-Century America," *Signs* 1, no. 1 (1975): 1–29.

13. Bonnie S. Anderson, *Joyous Greetings: The First International Women's Movement, 1830–1860* (New York: Oxford University Press, 2000); Leila Rupp, *Worlds of Women: The Making of an International Women's Movement* (Princeton: Princeton University Press, 1997).

14. Sigmund Freud, "Mourning and Melancholia," in SE XIV: 243–58.

15. Ibid., 249.

16. Judith Butler, *Gender Trouble: Feminism and the Subversion of Identity* (New York: Routledge, 1990), 57–66.

17. For a trenchant analysis of the current state of women's studies, see Wendy Brown, "Women's Studies Unbound: Revolution, Mourning, Politics," *parallax* 9, no. 2 (2003): 3–16.

18. Scott, Evans, Cahn, and Faue, "Women's History in the New Millennium: A Conversation across Three Generations; Part II," 199–220.

19. Jacques Lacan, "Subversion of the Subject and the Dialectic of Desire in the Freudian Unconscious," in Jacques Lacan, *Écrits*, trans. Alan Sheridan (New York: W. W. Norton, 1977), 292–324. See also the entry on "Desire" in Dylan Evans, *An Introductory Dictionary of Lacanian Psychoanalysis* (London: Routledge, 1996), 37.

20. Jacques Lacan, *The Four Fundamental Concepts of Psycho-Analysis* (New York: W. W. Norton, 1981), 154.

21. Wendy Brown and Janet Halley, eds., Introduction, *Left Legalism/Left Critique* (Durham: Duke University Press, 2002), 28.

22. Joan Wallach Scott, *Only Paradoxes to Offer: French Feminists and the Rights of Man* (Cambridge: Harvard University Press, 1996).

23. Scott, Evans, Cahn, and Faue, "Women's History in the New Millennium: A Conversation across Three Generations; Part II," 205.

24. Wendy Brown, *States of Injury: Power and Freedom in Late Modernity* (Princeton: Princeton University Press, 1995).

25. Gayle Rubin, "The Traffic in Women: Notes on the 'Political Economy' of Sex," in *Toward an Anthropology of Women*, ed. Rayna R. Reiter (New York: Monthly Review Press, 1975), 157–210.

26. Natalie Zemon Davis, " 'Women's History' in Transition: The European Case," *Feminist Studies* 3, nos. 3–4 (1976): 83–103.

27. The collected papers of the conference appear in Carole S. Vance, ed., *Pleasure and Danger* (New York: Routledge, 1984).

28. Denise Riley, *"Am I That Name?" Feminism and the Category of "Women" in History* (London: Macmillan, 1988).

29. Ann Snitow, "A Gender Diary," in *Conflicts in Feminism*, ed. Marianne Hirsch and Evelyn Fox Keller (London: Routledge, 1990), 9–43.

30. Evelyn Brooks Higginbotham, "African-American Women's History and the Metalanguage of Race," in *Feminism and History*, ed. Joan Wallach Scott (Oxford: Oxford University Press, 1996), 202.

31. Afsaneh Najmabadi, "Teaching and Research in Unavailable Intersections,"

differences 9, no. 3 (1997): 76, note 6. See also Afsaneh Najmabadi, *Women with Mustaches and Men without Beards: Gender and Sexual Anxieties of Iranian Modernity* (Berkeley: University of California Press, 2005).

32. Quoted in Wendy Brown, *Politics out of History* (Princeton: Princeton University Press, 2001), 41.

33. See Ellen Rooney, "Discipline and Vanish: Feminism, the Resistance to Theory, and the Politics of Cultural Studies," *differences* 2, no. 3 (1990): 14–28.

34. Robyn Wiegman, "What Ails Feminist Criticism? A Second Opinion," *Critical Inquiry* 25, no. 2 (1999); and "Feminism, Institutionalism, and the Idiom of Failure," *differences* 11, no. 3 (1999–2000): 107–36.

35. Ann Snitow, Christine Stansell, and Sharon Thompson, eds., *The Powers of Desire: The Politics of Sexuality* (New York: Monthly Review Press, 1983).

36. Brown and Halley, Introduction, *Left Legalism/Left Critique*, 33.

37. Quoted in Carlos Parada and Maicar Förlag, Greek Mythology Link website, "Muses," 1997, http://www.maicar.com/GML/MUSES.html.

2. Fantasy Echo

1. Joan Wallach Scott, "Multiculturalism and the Politics of Identity," in *The Identity in Question*, ed. John Rajchman (New York: Routledge, 1995), 3–12.

2. Denise Riley, *"Am I That Name?" Feminism and the Category of "Women" in History* (London: Macmillan, 1988).

3. Eric J. Hobsbawm, "Inventing Traditions," in *The Invention of Tradition*, ed. Eric J. Hobsbawm and Terence O. Ranger (Cambridge: Cambridge University Press, 1983), 1–14.

4. Joan Wallach Scott, *Only Paradoxes to Offer: French Feminists and the Rights of Man* (Cambridge: Harvard University Press, 1996).

5. For an example, see R. G. Collingwood, *The Idea of History* (New York: Oxford University Press, 1956).

6. Jean Laplanche and Jean-Bertrand Pontalis, "Fantasy and the Origins of Sexuality," in *Formations of Fantasy*, ed. Victor Burgin, James Donald, and Cora Kaplan (London: Routledge, 1986), 5–34.

7. Ibid., 26.

8. Denise Riley, *The Words of Selves: Identification, Solidarity, Irony* (Stanford: Stanford University Press, 2000), 13.

9. Sigmund Freud, "'A Child Is Being Beaten': A Contribution to the Study of the Origin of Sexual Perversions," in SE XVII: 175–203.

10. Slavoj Žižek, *The Plague of Fantasies* (London: Verso, 1997), 26–27.

11. Jacqueline Rose, *States of Fantasy* (Oxford: Oxford University Press, 1996), 3.

12. Sean Homer, "The Frankfurt School, the Father and the Social Fantasy," *New Formations* 38 (Summer 1999): 78–90.

13. J. Scott, *Only Paradoxes to Offer.*

14. Quoted in John Hollander, *The Figure of Echo: A Mode of Allusion in Milton*

and After (Berkeley: University of California Press, 1981), 25. See Ovid, *Metamorphoses*, trans. Frank Justus Miller and ed. G. P. Goold (Cambridge: Cambridge University Press, 1977), 150–51.

15. Quoted in Hollander, *The Figure of Echo*, 25.

16. Quoted in Claire Nouvet, "An Impossible Response: The Disaster of Narcissus," *Yale French Studies* no. 79 (1991): 113.

17. Nouvet rejects as too narrow and too literal a reading of Ovid a possible feminist interpretation that would take the bodiless Echo, who cannot initiate sound, as the representative of the feminine—derivative and secondary—in Western culture. See ibid., 109. See also Naomi Segal, "Echo and Narcissus," in *Between Feminism and Psychoanalysis*, ed. Teresa Brennan (New York: Routledge, 1989), 168–85. Denise Riley has an important discussion of Echo in terms of irony and identity. Denise Riley, *Words of Selves*, especially 155–61.

18. Julia Kristeva, "Stabat Mater," in *The Kristeva Reader*, trans. Leon S. Roudiez, ed. Toril Moi (New York: Columbia University Press, 1986), 161.

19. Miglena Nikolchina, *Matricide in Language: Writing Theory in Kristeva and Woolf* (New York: Other Press, 2004).

20. Olympe de Gouges, *Déclaration des droits de la femme et de la citoyenne* (Paris, 1791), article X, 9.

21. Quoted in Béatrice Slama, "Écrits de femmes pendant la révolution," in *Les femmes et la révolution française: actes du colloque international, 12–13–14 avril 1989*, ed. Marie-France Brive (Toulouse, France: Presses universitaires du Mirail, 1989), 2:297.

22. E. Lairtullier, *Les Femmes célèbres de 1789 à 1795, et leur influence dans la révolution, pour servir de suite et de complément à toutes les histoires de la révolution française* (Paris, 1840), 2:140.

23. Jeanne Deroin, "Compte-rendu du résultat de notre appel aux électeurs," *L'opinion des femmes*, supplement to no. 4 (May 7, 1849), n.p.

24. Quoted in Michèle Serrière, "Jeanne Deroin," in *Femmes et travail* (Paris: Matinsart, 1981), 26.

25. Madeleine Pelletier, *La femme vierge* (Paris: Valentin Bresle, 1933), 186.

26. Lily Braun, *Memoiren einer Sozialistin: Lehrjahre*, vol. 2, *Gesammelte Werke* (Berlin: Hermann Klemm, 1923), 2:455.

27. Joan Rivière, "Womanliness as a Masquerade," *International Journal of Psychoanalysis* 8 (1927): 304.

28. Jeanne Deroin, *Almanach des femmes, pour 1853* (London: J. Watson, 1853), 73.

29. Quoted in Christine Bard, *Les filles de Marianne: histoire des féminismes 1914–1940* (Paris: Fayard, 1995), 45.

30. Madeleine Pelletier, *La femme en lutte pour ses droits* (Paris, 1908), 37.

31. See, for example, Donna Bassin, Margaret Honey, and Meryle Maher Kaplan, eds., *Representations of Motherhood* (New Haven: Yale University Press, 1994).

32. Quoted in Jane Addams, Emily G. Balch, and Alice Hamilton, *Women at the*

Hague: The International Congress of Women and Its Results (1915; New York: Garland, 1972), 143.

33. Hanna Segal, *Introduction to the Work of Melanie Klein* (New York: Basic, 1964).

34. See, for example, Nancy J. Chodorow, *The Power of Feelings: Personal Meaning in Psychoanalysis, Gender, and Culture* (New Haven: Yale University Press, 1999).

35. Jacques Lacan, *On Feminine Sexuality: The Limits of Love and Knowledge*, trans. Bruce Fink (New York: W. W. Norton, 1998), 74.

36. Luce Irigaray, "The Bodily Encounter with the Mother," *The Irigaray Reader*, trans. David Macey, ed. Margaret Whitford (Oxford: Blackwell, 1991), 41.

37. Quoted in Susan K. Grogan, *French Socialism and Sexual Difference: Women and the New Society, 1803–44* (London: Macmillan, 1992), 187.

38. Quoted in ibid., 189.

39. Quoted in Michèle Riot-Sarcey, *La démocratie à l'épreuve des femmes: trois figures critiques du pouvoir, 1830–1848* (Paris: Albin Michel, 1994), 275.

40. Jeanne Deroin, *La voix des femmes*, March 28, 1848, n.p.

41. Quoted in Eileen Boris, "The Power of Motherhood: Black and White Activist Women Redefine the 'Political,'" *Yale Journal of Law and Feminism* 2 (1989): 36.

42. Quoted in Bard, *Les filles de Marianne*, 45.

43. Robin Morgan, "Introduction: Planetary Feminism: The Politics of the 21st Century," in *Sisterhood Is Global: The International Women's Movement Anthology*, compiled, edited, introduced, with a new preface by Robin Morgan (New York: Feminist Press, 1996), 36.

44. Irigaray, "The Bodily Encounter with the Mother," 63.

45. Steven C. Caton, "The Sheik," in *Noble Dreams, Wicked Pleasures: Orientalism in America, 1870–1930*, ed. Holly Edwards (Princeton: Princeton University Press, 2000), 99–117. See also Steven C. Caton, *Lawrence of Arabia: A Film's Anthropology* (Berkeley: University of California Press, 1999), 153, 208–9.

3. Feminist Reverberations

This chapter was first written as the keynote address for the Berkshire Conference on Women's History, June 2002.

1. Stanley Pargellis to Dorothy Ganfield Fowler, March 6, 1942, Papers of the Berkshire Conference of Women Historians, Schlesinger Library, Mc, 267, Radcliffe College, Harvard University.

2. Fowler to Pargellis, March 18, 1942, ibid.

3. Pargellis to Fowler, March 19, 1942, ibid.

4. Fowler to Pargellis, March 23, 1942, ibid.

5. Pargellis to Fowler, March 27, 1942, ibid.

6. Fowler to Pargellis, April 22, 1942, ibid.

7. Stanley Pargellis, ed., *The Quest for Political Unity in World History*, vol. 3, *Annual Report of the American Historical Association for the Year 1942* (Washington: US Government Printing Office, 1944).

8. Wendy Brown, "Power without Logic without Marx," in Wendy Brown, *Politics out of History* (Princeton: Princeton University Press, 2001), 62–90.

9. I would now add Iraq and Iran to the list.

10. Clifford Geertz, "The World in Pieces: Culture and Politics at the End of the Century," in Clifford Geertz, *Available Light: Anthropological Reflections on Philosophical Topics* (Princeton: Princeton University Press, 2000), 218–63.

11. Denise Riley, *The Words of Selves: Identification, Solidarity, Irony* (Stanford: Stanford University Press, 2000), 176.

12. Bernard Lewis, "The Revolt of Islam," *New Yorker*, November 19, 2001; Samuel P. Huntington, *The Clash of Civilizations and the Remaking of World Order* (New York: Simon and Schuster, 1996).

13. Talal Asad, *On Suicide Bombing* (New York: Columbia University Press, 2007).

14. Radio address by Laura Bush, November 17, 2001 (http://www.presidency.ucsb.edu).

15. Quoted in Kathleen T. Rhem, "Women's Rights a Priority; Humanitarian Aid Improves," American Forces Press Service (http://www.defense.gov/news/newsarticle.aspx?id=44432).

16. Asia Source Interview with Lila Abu-Lughod, "Women and Islam: An Interview with Lila Abu-Lughod," February 2002. Interview by Nermeen Shaikh. Available from http://www.ciaonet.org/wps/abl02/index.html.

17. Iris Marion Young, "The Logics of Masculinist Protection: Reflections on the Current Security State," *Signs* 29, no. 1 (2003): 4.

18. Ibid., 9.

19. Fatima Gailani, comments at a commencement forum on "Women in Afghanistan," Brown University, Providence, Rhode Island, May 25, 2002.

20. Anna Tsing, "Transitions as Translations," in *Transitions, Environments, Translations: Feminism in International Politics*, ed. Joan Wallach Scott, Cora Kaplan, and Debra Keates (New York: Routledge, 1997), 253.

21. See chapter 2.

22. Quoted in Alan Cowell, "In 'Hidden Vote' for Le Pen, French Bared Growing Discontent," *New York Times*, May 3, 2002.

23. Judith Butler, *Gender Trouble: Feminism and the Subversion of Identity* (New York: Routledge, 1990), 7.

24. Miglena Nikolchina, "Translating Gender: The Bulgarian Case," *The Making of European Women's Studies*, ed. Rosi Braidotti (Utrecht, the Netherlands: ATHENA 2001), 3:92–94.

25. Laura Engelstein, "Culture, Culture Everywhere: Interpretations of Modern Russia, across the 1991 Divide," *Kritika* 2, no. 2 (2001): 363–93.

26. Quoted in François Dosse, *History of Structuralism* (Minneapolis: University of Minnesota Press, 1997), 2:55.

27. Miglena Nikolchina, "The Seminar: *Mode d'emploi*," *differences* 13, no. 1 (2002): 96–127.

28. Catharine A. MacKinnon, Part III, "Through the Bosnian Lens," in *Are Women Human? And Other International Dialogues* (Cambridge: Harvard University Press, 2006), 141–236. For a critique of MacKinnon, see Vesna Kesic, "Response to Catherine [*sic*] MacKinnon's article "Turning Rape into Pornography: Postmodern Genocide," *Hastings Women's Law Journal* 5 (1994): 267–80.

29. This and what follows is quoted from or based on the Women in Black website (http://womeninblack.org).

30. Haresh Kapoor, "Women in Black lay down in front of tanks in Ramallah," press release, December 23, 2001 (http://mail-archive.com/kominform@lists .eunet.fi/msg10982.html); Tim Kingston, "FBI Casting Wide Net in Sept. 11 Attack Investigation," *San Francisco Bay Guardian*, October 14, 2001 (http:// www.wluml.org/node/650).

31. Cynthia Cockburn, "Being Able to Say Neither/Nor," notes for a talk at a meeting organized by Peace Brigades International and the National Peace Council, London, April 14, 1999 (http://cynthiacockburn.typepad.com/Blogneithernor.pdf).

32. "Women in Black" (http://womeninblack.org/en/about).

33. Jasmina Tešanović, *Me and My Multicultural Street* (Belgrade, Serbia: Feministicka, 2001), 46.

34. Ibid., 43.

35. I met Tešanović at a conference in Dubrovnik after I had given the talk that this chapter is based on. It was a very moving experience, another one of those reverberations I was trying to write about.

36. Tešanović, *Me and My Multicultural Street*, 50–51.

37. Ibid., 51–52. See also Ghislaine Glasson Deschaumes and Svetlana Slapsak, eds., *Femmes des Balkans pour la paix: itinéraires d'une action militante à travers les frontières* (Paris: Transeuropéennes/RCE, 2002).

38. There are other examples of solidarities based on difference. In France, the Collectif des Féministes pour l'Egalité brings together Muslim women in head scarves and secular women (Muslim and "native" Frenchwomen) under the banner of an end to domination of all kinds: "no forced wearing of head scarves, no forced removal of head scarves" is their motto. See Ismahane Chouder, Malika Latrèche, and Pierre Tevanian, *Les filles voilées parlent* (Paris: La Fabrique, 2008). In Turkey, a similar, though less formal, alliance has emerged between secular and religious women: "We build our community by transcending dichotomies despite dichotomies and through dichotomies. We build our community by transcending social identities despite social identities and through social identities." See "We Care for Each Other," first petition, February 29, 2008, and second petition, September 26, 2008 (http://www.birbirimizesahipcikiyoruz.blogspot .com/). The process of negotiation of differences is not easy; in both instances, the question of supporting homosexuals against discrimination creates tremendous, unresolved difficulties.

39. A recent example of "feminist reverberations" of this kind is the group called La Barbe (the beard) in France. Founded in 2008 and consisting of around a hundred women, the group engages in actions (inspired by Guerilla Girls, Act UP, Yes Men, and Lesbian Avengers) that protest the exclusion of women in politics, education, business, etc. A small group arrives at, say, a stockholders meeting, and, donning obviously fake beards, congratulates the group on the absence of women among them. They have managed to get press coverage (one can find them on YouTube as well) for their ironic interventions and denunciations of sexism. The first such actions were developed in a different context in Turkey. There is a group called Las Bigotonas, founded in 2009, in Mexico. And there are efforts to adopt this strategy in the Czech Republic. See the Facebook page for La-Barbe-groupe-daction-féministe. See also www.labarbelabarbe.org.

40. Quoted in Christine Bard, *Les filles de Marianne: histoire des féminismes 1914–1940* (Paris: Fayard, 1995), 45.

41. For recent work on global feminist movements, see Peggy Antrobus, *The Global Women's Movement: Origins, Issues, and Strategies* (London: Zed, 2004); Myra Marx Ferree and Aili Mari Tripp, eds., *Global Feminism: Transnational Women's Activism, Organizing, and Human Rights* (New York: New York University Press, 2006); Inderpal Grewal, *Transnational America: Feminisms, Diasporas, Neoliberalisms* (Durham: Duke University Press, 2005); Valentine Moghadam, *Globalizing Women: Transnational Feminist Networks* (Baltimore: Johns Hopkins University Press, 2005); Chandra Talpade Mohanty, *Feminism without Borders: Decolonizing Theory, Practicing Solidarity* (Durham: Duke University Press, 2003).

4. Sexularism

1. After I wrote this chapter I was alerted to an online lecture by Ann Pelligrini at the University of California, Santa Barbara, called "Sexularism: Religious Freedom, American Style" (http://www.uctv.tv/search-details.aspx?showID=15371). Pellegrini's use of the term refers to the ways in which sex—especially the sexual moralities associated with religious teachings—continue to influence modern secular societies. See also Janet R. Jakobsen and Ann Pellegrini, *Love the Sin: Sexual Regulation and the Limits of Religious Tolerance* (New York: New York University Press, 2003).

2. Hence in *Women and Human Development: The Capabilities Approach* (Cambridge: Cambridge University Press, 2001), Martha Nussbaum argues that "opportunities for sexual satisfaction are an important aspect of bodily integrity, a central human functional capability," and that the secular state becomes the place where "the truly human" is defined (78–79).

3. Quoted in Dominic McGoldrick, *Human Rights and Religion: The Islamic Debate in Europe* (Portland, Ore.: Hart, 2006), 89. On the French head scarf debates, see Joan Wallach Scott, *The Politics of the Veil.* (Princeton: Princeton

University Press, 2007). See also John R. Bowen, *Why the French Don't Like Headscarves: Islam, the State, and Public Space* (Princeton: Princeton University Press, 2006).

4. Quoted in McGoldrick, *Human Rights and Religion*, 128; see also 206.

5. Quoted in ibid., 266.

6. Alexis de Tocqueville, *Souvenirs* (Paris: Gallimard, 1964), 129.

7. Madelyn Gutwirth, *The Twilight of the Goddesses: Women and Representation in the French Revolutionary Era* (New Brunswick, N.J.: Rutgers University Press, 1992), 275.

8. Ibid., 364.

9. Ibid., 365.

10. Ibid.

11. Richard Cobb, *Les armées révolutionnaires: instrument de la terreur dans les départements, avril 1793–Floréal an II* (Paris: Mouton, 1961–63), 1:450.

12. Charles Taylor, *A Secular Age* (Cambridge: Harvard University Press, 2007), 167.

13. Pierre Rosenvallon, *Le modèle politique français: la société civile contre le jacobinisme de 1789 à nos jours* (Paris: Seuil, 2004), 47–55.

14. Talal Asad, *Formations of the Secular: Christianity, Islam, Modernity* (Stanford: Stanford University Press, 2003), 59.

15. Ibid., 25.

16. Hussein Ali Agrama, "Secularism, Sovereignty, Indeterminancy: Is Egypt a Secular or a Religious State?," *Comparative Studies in Society and History* 52, no. 3 (2010): 519.

17. Carol Christ, "Victorian Masculinity and the Angel in the House," in *A Widening Sphere: Changing Roles of Victorian Women*, ed. Martha Vicinus (Bloomington: Indiana University Press, 1977), 146–62; Gay Gullickson, *Unruly Women of Paris: Images of the Commune* (Ithaca: Cornell University Press, 1996).

18. Quoted in Cobb, *Les armées révolutionnaires*, 450.

19. Thomas Laqueur, *Making Sex: Body and Gender from the Greeks to Freud* (Cambridge: Harvard University Press, 1990), 193.

20. Darlene Levy, Harriet Applewhite, and Mary Johnson, eds. *Women in Revolutionary Paris, 1789–1795: Selected Documents*, translated with notes and commentary by the editors (Urbana: University of Illinois Press, 1979), 215.

21. This is not a new insight, but the fruit of second-wave feminist historical research, which is sometimes forgotten in the context of current debates about Muslims.

22. Carole Pateman, *The Sexual Contract* (London: Polity, 1988), 6.

23. For information on women in national legislatures around the world, see statistics compiled by the Inter-Parliamentary Union (http://www.ipu.org/wmn-e/classif.htm).

24. Nancy Cott, *The Grounding of Modern Feminism* (New Haven: Yale University Press, 1987), 185–87.

25. Wendy Brown, "The 'Jewish Question' and the 'Woman Question,'" in *Going Public: Feminism and the Shifting Boundaries of the Private Sphere*, ed. Joan Wallach Scott and Debra Keates (Urbana: University of Illinois Press, 2004), 36.

26. Eric Fassin, "The Rise and Fall of Sexual Politics: A Transatlantic Comparison," *Public Culture* 18, no. 1 (2006): 79–92; and "L'empire du genre. L'histoire politique ambiguë d'un outil conceptuel," *L'homme*, nos. 187–88, (juillet–décembre 2008), 375–92.

27. Quoted in Roslyne Bachelot and Geneviève Fraisse, *Deux femmes au royaume des hommes* (Paris: Hachette, 1999), 12.

28. Conseil d'Etat, *Réflexions sur la laïcité* (Paris: Conseil d'Etat, 2004), 295.

29. Ibid., 341.

30. Julia Clancy-Smith, "Islam, Gender and Identities in the Making of French Algeria, 1830–1962," in *Domesticating the Empire: Race, Gender, and Family Life in French and Dutch Colonialism*, ed. Julia Clancy-Smith and Frances Gouda (Charlottesville: University of Virginia Press, 1998), 154–55.

31. Paul Silverstein, *Algeria in France: Transpolitics, Race, and Nation* (Bloomington: Indiana University Press, 2004), 52.

32. Todd Shepard, *The Invention of Decolonization: The Algerian War and the Remaking of France* (Ithaca: Cornell University Press, 2006), 186–92.

33. Quoted in Eddy Souffrant, "To Conquer the Veil: Woman as a Critique of Liberalism," in *Fanon: A Critical Reader*, ed. Lewis Gordon, T. D. Sharpley-Whiting, and Renée White (Cambridge, Mass.: Wiley-Blackwell, 1996), 177.

34. Frantz Fanon, "Algeria Unveiled," in Frantz Fanon, *A Dying Colonialism*, trans. Haakon Chevalier (New York: Grove, 1965), 35–67.

35. Marnia Lazreg, *The Eloquence of Silence: Algerian Women in Question* (New York: Routledge, 1994), 49; Anouar Majid, "The Politics of Feminism in Islam," *Signs* 23, no. 2 (1998): 351.

36. Afsaneh Najmabadi, "Gender and the Sexual Politics of Public Visibility in Iranian Modernity," in *Going Public: Feminism and the Shifting Boundaries of the Private Sphere*, ed. Joan Wallach Scott and Debra Keates (Urbana: University of Illinois Press, 2004), 60.

37. Richard Stites, *The Women's Liberation Movement in Russia: Feminism, Nihilism, and Bolshevism, 1860–1930* (Princeton: Princeton University Press, 1978), 327.

38. Riva Kastoryano, "Religion and Incorporation: Islam in France," paper presented at the Annual Meeting of the International Studies Association, New York, February 2009, 12.

39. Kathleen Sands, "Feminisms and Secularisms," in *Secularisms*, ed. Janet R. Jakobsen and Ann Pellegrini (Durham: Duke University Press, 2008), 315.

40. Phyllis Mack, "Religion, Feminism, and the Problem of Agency: Reflections on Eighteenth-Century Quakerism," in *Women, Gender, and Enlightenment*, ed. Sarah Knott and Barbara Taylor (Houndmills, Basingstoke, Hampshire: Palgrave Macmillan, 2005), 434.

41. Ibid., 439.

42. Saba Mahmood, *Politics of Piety: The Islamic Revival and the Feminist Subject* (Princeton: Princeton University Press, 2005), 15.

43. Ibid., 17.

44. Mack, "Religion, Feminism, and the Problem of Agency," 439.

45. Ibid., 454.

46. Mahmood, *Politics of Piety*, 32.

47. Asad, *Formations of the Secular*, 229–30.

48. Mahmood, *Politics of Piety*, 25.

49. Mack, "Religion, Feminism, and the Problem of Agency," 445.

50. Mahmood, *Politics of Piety*, 37.

51. Ibid., 155.

52. Ismahane Chouder, Malika Latrèche, and Pierre Tevanian, *Les filles voilées parlent* (Paris: La Fabrique, 2008), 30.

53. Ibid., 42.

54. The anthropologist Mayanthi Fernando argues that French Muslim girls in hijab face an impossible situation. Their religious commitments are realized by wearing the hijab, and these commitments cannot be privatized as the state requires. Yet this is a freely chosen religious obligation. Since French secularism cannot accept the idea of free choice as a choice to submit, the girls are treated either as dishonest individuals or as victims of communal pressure. See Mayanthi Fernando, "Reconfiguring Freedom: Muslim Piety and the Limits of Secular Public Discourse and Law," *American Ethnologist* 37, no. 1 (2010): 19–35.

55. Chouder, Latrèche, and Tevanian, *Les filles voilées parlent*, 127.

56. Ibid., 288.

57. Sabrina Tavernise, "Youthful Voice Stirs Challenge to Secular Turks," *New York Times*, October 14, 2008.

58. Nilüfer Göle, *Interpénétrations: L'Islam et l'Europe* (Paris: Galaade, 2005), 27. Later in the book, she writes: "Today, the return to the Islamic veil signifies the adoption—voluntary or imposed depending on the case—of a sign of 'stigma' on the part of the women who wear it. They are seeking to transform it into a sign of prestige" (123).

59. Tavernise, "Youthful Voice Stirs Challenge to Secular Turks," *New York Times*, October 14, 2008.

60. Chouder, Latrèche, and Tevanian, *Les filles voilées parlent*, 310–11.

61. Ibid., 327.

62. Ibid., 238. For a similar Turkish example, see chapter 3 of this book, note 38.

63. European Court of Human Rights, *Grand Chamber Judgment: Leyla Şahin v. Turkey*, dissenting opinion of Judge Tulkens, 2005, 15.

64. Asad, *Formations of the Secular*, 197.

65. Chouder, Latrèche, and Tevanian, *Les filles voilées parlent*, 53.

66. Dounia Bouzar and Saïda Kada, *L'une voilée, l'autre pas: Le témoinage de deux musulmanes françaises* (Paris: Albin Michel, 2003), 58–59.

67. Chouder, Latrèche, and Tevanian, *Les filles voilées parlent*, 217.

68. I am aware that there are queer theorists who strongly object to this view.

As Michael Warner put it to me, "coming from the milieu of queer and trans-[gender] theory, it's hard for me to take at face value the kind of psychoanalytically rooted discourse about dimorphic sexual difference that is so common in French debates, just as it's hard for me to think that desire is just the same for everybody" (personal e-mail correspondence, August 26, 2010). I would argue that there's a difference between the literalizing of "dimorphic sexual difference" by some psychoanalysts and popularizers of psychoanalytic discourse—the notion that anatomy is destiny, to put it briefly—and the theories of Freud and Lacan and their followers that I have cited. For these theorists, sexual difference is a problem, not a prescription, and the fantasies it gives rise to permit all manner of identities, identifications, and practices: queer, straight, transgender, and others. And desire, far from being assumed to be "the same for everybody," is taken to be a process whose direction and substance are open questions to be examined contextually and specifically.

69. Bruce Fink, *The Lacanian Subject: Between Language and Jouissance* (Princeton: Princeton University Press, 1995), 104.

70. Jacques Lacan, *On Feminine Sexuality: The Limits of Love and Knowledge*, trans. Bruce Fink (New York: W. W. Norton, 1998); and *Ecrits*, trans. Alan Sheridan (New York: W. W. Norton, 1977).

71. Lacan, *On Feminine Sexuality*, 113.

72. Ibid., 112.

5. French Seduction Theory

1. Philippe Raynaud, "Les femmes et la civilité: aristocratie et passions révolutionnaires," *Le Débat*, no. 57 (November–December 1989), 182.

2. Mona Ozouf, "Un essai de Claude Habib: séduire est-il un art français?," *Le Nouvel Observateur*, November 9, 2006.

3. Claude Habib, *Galanterie française* (Paris: Gallimard, 2006), 410.

4. Mona Ozouf, *Les mots des femmes: essai sur la singularité française* (Paris: Gallimard, 1995).

5. Eric Fassin, "National Identities and Transnational Intimacies: Sexual Democracy and the Politics of Immigration in Europe," *Public Culture* 22, no. 3 (2010): 519.

6. Jacques Lacan, *The Ethics of Psychoanalysis, 1959–1960*, trans. Dennis Porter (New York: W. W. Norton, 1992), 143.

7. Eric J. Hobsbawm and Terence O. Ranger, eds., *The Invention of Tradition* (Cambridge: Cambridge University Press, 1983); Benedict Anderson, *Imagined Communities: Reflections on the Origin and Spread of Nationalism* (London: Verso, 1983); Geoff Eley and Ronald G. Suny, eds., *Becoming National* (New York: Oxford University Press, 1996).

8. Raynaud, "Les femmes et la civilité," 181.

9. Ibid., 185.

10. Raynaud, "Les femmes et la civilité," 181.

11. Ozouf, *Les mots des femmes*, 323, 329.

12. Quoted in ibid., 326.

13. Ozouf, "Un essai de Claude Habib."

14. Claude Habib, *Consentement Amoureux* (Paris: Hachette, 1998).

15. Mona Ozouf, "A propos du 'Consentement Amoureux': les douces lois de l'attraction," *Le Nouvel Observateur*, November 26, 1998.

16. Alain Corbin, "Faites galant," *L'Express*, December 7, 2006.

17. Quoted in Raynaud, "Les femmes et la civilité," 182.

18. Habib, *Galanterie française*, 51.

19. Ibid.

20. Ibid., 55.

21. Quoted in Ozouf, *Les mots des femmes*, 355.

22. Ibid., 347.

23. Habib, *Galanterie française*, 411.

24. Eliane Viennot, *La France, les femmes, et le pouvoir*, 2 vols. (Paris: Perrin, 2006 and 2008). See also Eliane Viennot, ed., *La démocratie à la française ou les femmes indésirables* (Paris: Cahiers du CEDREF, 2002).

25. Viennot, *La France, les femmes, et le pouvoir*, 1:58.

26. Choderlos de Laclos, *Les liaisons dangereuses*, trans. Douglas Parmée (Oxford: Oxford University Press, 2008), 163.

27. Ibid.

28. Ibid., 161–62.

29. Ibid., 292.

30. Sigmund Freud, *Totem and Taboo*, SE XIII:1–163. An overview, with many eighteenth-century citations, can be found in Lynn Hunt, *The Family Romance of the French Revolution* (Berkeley: University of California Press, 1992). See also Carole Pateman, *The Sexual Contract* (London: Polity, 1988).

31. A good discussion of the uncertainty surrounding transitions from absolute monarchy to more democratic forms is found in Judith Surkis, "Carnival Balls and Penal Codes: Body Politics in July Monarchy France," *History of the Present* 1, no. 1 (2011): 59–83.

32. Jacques Lacan, "Desire and the Interpretation of Desire in Hamlet," *Yale French Studies*, no. 55–56 (1977): 11–52. "Replace the word 'king' with the word 'phallus,'" Lacan writes of Hamlet's relationship to Claudius, who is both his uncle and his king, "and you'll see that that's really the point—the body is bound up in this matter of the phallus—and how—but the phallus, on the contrary is bound to nothing: it always slips through your fingers" (52).

33. Jacques Lacan, "The Signification of the Phallus," in Jacques Lacan, *Écrits*, trans. Alan Sheridan (New York: W. W. Norton, 1977), 281–91.

34. Slavoj Žižek, *The Sublime Object of Ideology* (London: Verso, 1989); and *The Plague of Fantasies* (London: Verso, 1997).

35. Jacques Lacan, *On Feminine Sexuality: The Limits of Love and Knowledge,*

trans. Bruce Fink (New York: W. W. Norton, 1998). See also Bruce Fink, *The Lacanian Subject: Between Language and Jouissance* (Princeton: Princeton University Press, 1995).

36. Habib, *Galanterie française*, 55.

37. Ibid., 421.

38. Ibid., 46.

39. Ibid., 44, 51, 93, 77.

40. Mona Ozouf, "A Propos du 'Consentement Amoureux': les douces lois de l'attraction," *Le Nouvel Observateur*, November 26, 1998.

41. Ibid., 426.

42. Quoted in ibid., 427.

43. Ozouf, *Les mots des femmes*, 381.

44. Habib, *Galanterie française*, 77.

45. Ozouf, *Les mots des femmes*, 385.

46. Habib, *Galanterie française*, 417.

47. Raynaud, "Les femmes et la civilité," 180.

48. Ibid.

49. Habib, *Galanterie française*, 419.

50. Jacques Julliard, editorial, *Le Nouvel Observateur*, 2–8 January 1997.

51. Ibid., 25.

52. Ibid., 24.

53. Habib, *Galanterie française*, 432–33.

54. Ibid., 421.

55. Ozouf, *Les mots des femmes*, 351.

56. Ibid., 360.

57. "Claude Habib," *Les Echos*, June 8, 2007 (www.lesechos.fr/luxe/people/300180664-claude-habib.htm).

58. Ozouf, *Les Mots des femmes*, 383.

59. Habib, *Galanterie française*, 412.

60. Ibid.

61. Ozouf, "Un essai de Claude Habib."

62. Habib, *Galanterie française*, 412–14.

63. Joan Wallach Scott, *The Politics of the Veil* (Princeton: Princeton University Press, 2007). See also Chahla Chafiq and Farhad Khoskrokavar, *Femmes sous le voile face à la loi islamique* (Paris: Félin, 1995).

64. Habib, *Galanterie française*, 412.

65. Ozouf, *Les mots des femmes*, 327.

66. Ibid.

67. Jean Baudrillard, *Seduction*, trans. Brian Singer (New York: St. Martin's Press, 1990), 74.

Epilogue

1. Charles Bernheim and Claire Kahane, eds., *In Dora's Case: Freud, Hysteria, Feminism* (New York: Columbia University Press, 1985); Janet Malcolm, "J'appelle un chat un chat," *New Yorker*, April 27, 1978, 84–102.

2. Elizabeth Weed, "Feminist Psychoanalytic Literary Criticism," in *The Cambridge Companion to Feminist Literary Theory*, ed. Ellen Rooney (Cambridge: Cambridge University Press, 2006), 262.

3. Michel Foucault, *Foucault Live: Interviews, 1966–84*, trans. John Johnston, ed. Sylvère Lotringer (New York: Semiotext(e), 1989), 27. See also Thomas Flynn, "Foucault's Mapping of History," in *The Cambridge Companion to Foucault*, ed. Gary Gutting (Cambridge: Cambridge University Press, 1994), 28–46.

4. Michel Foucault, *The Archaeology of Knowledge*, trans. A. M. Sheridan Smith (New York: Harper and Row, 1972), 128.

5. Ibid., 129.

6. Jacques Derrida, *Archive Fever: A Freudian Impression*, trans. Eric Prenowitz (Chicago: University of Chicago Press, 1996).

7. Jill Lepore, "The Iceman," *New Yorker*, January 25, 2010, 27.

8. Jules Michelet quoted in Carolyn Steedman, *Dust: The Archive and Cultural History* (New Brunswick: Rutgers University Press, 2002), 27.

9. Ibid.

10. Steedman, *Dust*, 65.

11. Michel de Certeau, *Heterologies: Discourse on the Other*, trans. Brian Massumi (Minneapolis: University of Minnesota Press, 1996), 194.

12. Steedman, *Dust*, 38.

13. Quoted in ibid., 27–28.

14. Ibid.

15. Jacques Derrida, *Eyes of the University: Right to Philosophy 2*, trans. Jan Plug et al. (Stanford: Stanford University Press, 2004), 226–27.

16. Jean Laplanche cited in Steedman, *Dust*, 77.

17. Steedman, *Dust*, 83.

18. Foucault, *Archaeology of Knowledge*, 129.

Bibliography

Adams, Parveen, and Elizabeth Cowie, eds. *The Woman in Question: m/f.* Cambridge: MIT Press, 1992.

Adams, Parveen, and Jeffrey Minson. "The 'Subject' of Feminism." In *The Woman in Question,* edited by Parveen Adams and Elizabeth Cowie, 81–101. Cambridge: MIT Press, 1990.

Addams, Jane, Emily G. Balch, and Alice Hamilton. *Women at the Hague: The International Congress of Women and Its Results.* 1915. New York: Garland, 1972.

Agrama, Hussein Ali. "Secularism, Sovereignty, Indeterminancy: Is Egypt a Secular or a Religious State?" *Comparative Studies in Society and History* 52, no. 3 (2010): 495–523.

Althusser, Louis. "Ideology and Ideological State Apparatuses." In Louis Althusser, *Lenin and Philosophy, and Other Essays,* translated by Ben Brewster, 127–88. New York: Monthly Review Press, 1972.

Anderson, Benedict. *Imagined Communities: Reflections on the Origin and Spread of Nationalism.* London: Verso, 1983.

Anderson, Bonnie S. *Joyous Greetings: The First International Women's Movement, 1830–1860.* New York: Oxford University Press, 2000.

Antrobus, Peggy. *The Global Women's Movement: Origins, Issues, and Strategies.* London: Zed, 2004.

Asad, Talal. *Formations of the Secular: Christianity, Islam, Modernity.* Stanford: Stanford University Press, 2003.

——. *On Suicide Bombing.* New York: Columbia University Press, 2007.

Bachelot, Roslyne, and Geneviève Fraisse. *Deux femmes au royaume des hommes.* Paris: Hachette, 1999.

Banner, Lois, and Mary S. Hartman, eds. *Clio's Consciousness Raised: New Perspectives on the History of Women, Sex and Class in Women's History.* New York: Harper and Row, 1974.

Bard, Christine. *Les filles de Marianne: histoire des féminismes 1914–1940.* Paris: Fayard, 1995.

Bassin, Donna, Margaret Honey, and Meryle Maher Kaplan, eds. *Representations of Motherhood.* New Haven: Yale University Press, 1994.

Baudrillard, Jean. *Seduction.* Translated by Brian Singer. New York: St. Martin's, 1990.

Beauvoir, Simone de. *The Second Sex.* Translated by H. M. Parshley. New York: Random House, 1974.

Boris, Eileen. "The Power of Motherhood: Black and White Activist Women Redefine the 'Political.'" *Yale Journal of Law and Feminism* 2 (1989): 25–49.

Bouzar, Dounia, and Saïda Kada. *L'une voilée, l'autre pas: Le témoignage de deux musulmanes françaises.* Paris: Albin Michel, 2003.

Bowen, John R. *Why the French Don't Like Headscarves: Islam, the State, and Public Space.* Princeton: Princeton University Press, 2006.

Braun, Lily. *Memoiren einer Sozialistin: Lehrjahre.* Vol. 2, *Gesammelte Werke.* Berlin: Hermann Klemm, 1923.

Brown, Wendy. "Tolerance and Equality: 'The Jewish Question' and 'the Woman Question.'" In *Going Public: Feminism and the Shifting Boundaries of the Private Sphere,* edited by Joan Wallach Scott and Debra Keates, 15–42. Urbana: University of Illinois Press, 2004.

———. *Politics out of History.* Princeton: Princeton University Press, 2001.

———. *States of Injury: Power and Freedom in Late Modernity.* Princeton: Princeton University Press, 1995.

———. "Women's Studies Unbound: Revolution, Mourning, Politics." *parallax* 9, no. 2 (2003): 3–16.

Brown, Wendy, and Janet Halley, eds. *Left Legalism/Left Critique.* Durham: Duke University Press, 2002.

Burke, Peter. "Freud and Cultural History." *Psychoanalysis and History* 9, no. 1 (2007): 5–15.

Butler, Judith. *Bodies That Matter: On the Discursive Limits of "Sex."* New York: Routledge, 1993.

———. *Gender Trouble: Feminism and the Subversion of Identity.* New York: Routledge, 1990.

———. *The Psychic Life of Power: Theories in Subjection.* Stanford: Stanford University Press, 1997.

———. *Undoing Gender.* New York: Routledge, 2004.

Butler, Judith, and Elizabeth Weed, eds. *The Question of Gender: Engaging with Joan W. Scott's Critical Feminism.* Bloomington: Indiana University Press, 2012.

Caton, Steven C. *Lawrence of Arabia: A Film's Anthropology.* Berkeley: University of California Press, 1999.

———. "The Sheik." In *Noble Dreams, Wicked Pleasures: Orientalism in America, 1870–1930*, edited by Holly Edwards, 99–117. Princeton: Princeton University Press, 2000.

Certeau, Michel de. *Heterologies: Discourse on the Other.* Translated by Brian Massumi. Minneapolis: University of Minneapolis Press, 1996.

———. *The Writing of History.* Translated by Tom Conley. New York: Columbia University Press, 1988.

Chafiq, Chahla, and Farhad Khoskrokavar. *Femmes sous le voile face à la loi islamique.* Paris: Félin, 1995.

Chakrabarty, Dipesh. *Provincializing Europe: Postcolonial Thought and Historical Difference.* Princeton: Princeton University Press, 2000.

Chouder, Ismahane, Malika Latrèche, and Pierre Tevanian. *Les filles voilées parlent.* Paris: La Fabrique, 2008.

Christ, Carol. "Victorian Masculinity and the Angel in the House." In *A Widening Sphere: Changing Roles of Victorian Women*, edited by Martha Vicinus, 146–62. Bloomington: Indiana University Press, 1977.

Clancy-Smith, Julia. "Islam, Gender, and Identities in the Making of French Algeria, 1830–1962." In *Domesticating the Empire: Race, Gender, and Family Life in French and Dutch Colonialism*, edited by Julia Clancy-Smith and Frances Gouda, 154–74. Charlottesville: University of Virginia Press, 1998.

Cobb, Richard. *Les armées révolutionnaires: instrument de la terreur dans les départements, avril 1793–Floréal an II.* Paris: Mouton, 1961–63.

Collingwood, R. G. *The Idea of History.* New York: Oxford University Press, 1956.

Conseil d'Etat. *Réflexions sur la laïcité.* Paris: Conseil d'Etat, 2004.

Copjec, Joan. "Cutting Up." In *Between Feminism and Psychoanalysis*, edited by Teresa Brennan, 227–46. New York: Routledge, 1989.

———. *Read My Desire: Lacan against the Historicists.* Cambridge: MIT Press, 1996.

Cott, Nancy. *The Grounding of Modern Feminism.* New Haven: Yale University Press, 1987.

Davis, Natalie Zemon. " 'Women's History' in Transition: The European Case." *Feminist Studies* 3, nos. 3–4 (1976): 83–103.

Deroin, Jeanne. *Almanach des femmes, pour 1853.* London: J. Watson, 1853.

Derrida, Jacques. *Archive Fever: A Freudian Impression.* Translated by Eric Prenowitz. Chicago: University of Chicago Press, 1996.

———. *Eyes of the University: Right to Philosophy 2.* Translated by Jan Plug et al. Stanford: Stanford University Press, 2004.

———. "Women in the Beehive: A Seminar." In *Men in Feminism*, edited by Alice Jardine and Paul Smith, 189–203. New York: Methuen, 1987.

Deschaumes, Ghislaine Glasson, and Svetlana Slapsak, eds. *Femmes des Balkans pour la paix: itinéraires d'une militante à travers les frontières.* Paris: Transeuropéennes/RCE, 2002.

Dosse, François. *History of Structuralism.* 2 vols. Minneapolis: University of Minnesota Press, 1997.

Duparc, François. *L'image sur le divan.* Paris: L'Harmattan, 1995.

———. "Secondary Revision." In *International Dictionary of Psychoanalysis,* 3 vols., ed. Alain de Mijolla, 3:1558–60. Framington Hills, Mich.: Thomson Gale, 2005.

Eley, Geoff, and Ronald G. Suny, eds. *Becoming National.* New York: Oxford University Press, 1996.

Engelstein, Laura. "Culture, Culture Everywhere: Interpretations of Modern Russia, across the 1991 Divide." *Kritika* 2, no. 2 (2001): 363–93.

Eribon, Didier. *Echapper à la psychanalyse.* Paris: Léo Scheer, 2005.

———. *Hérésies: Essais sur la théorie de la sexualité.* Paris: Fayard, 2003.

European Court of Human Rights. Grand Chamber Judgment. "Leyla Şahin v. Turkey." Dissenting opinion of Judge Tulkens. 2005.

Evans, Dylan. *An Introductory Dictionary of Lacanian Psychoanalysis.* London: Routledge, 1996.

Fanon, Frantz. "Algeria Unveiled." In Frantz Fanon, *A Dying Colonialism,* 35–67. Translated by Haakon Chevalier. New York: Grove, 1965.

Fassin, Eric. "L'empire du genre. L'histoire politique ambiguë d'un outil conceptuel." *L'homme,* nos. 187–88 (juillet–décembre 2008): 375–92.

———. "National Identities and Transnational Intimacies: Sexual Democracy and the Politics of Immigration in Europe." *Public Culture* 22, no. 3 (2010): 507–29.

———. "The Rise and Fall of Sexual Politics. A Transatlantic Comparison." *Public Culture* 18, no. 1 (2006): 79–92.

Fernando, Mayanthi. "Reconfiguring Freedom: Muslim Piety and the Limits of Secular Public Discourse and Law." *American Ethnologist* 37, no. 1 (2010): 19–35.

Ferree, Myra Marx, and Aili Mari Tripp, eds. *Global Feminism: Transnational Women's Activism, Organizing, and Human Rights.* New York: New York University Press, 2006.

Fink, Bruce. *The Lacanian Subject: Between Language and Jouissance.* Princeton: Princeton University Press, 1995.

Flynn, Thomas. "Foucault's Mapping of History." In *The Cambridge Companion to Foucault,* edited by Gary Gutting, 28–46. Cambridge: Cambridge University Press, 1994.

"Forum on Transnational Sexualities." *American Historical Review* 114, no. 4 (2009): 1250–353.

Foucault, Michel. *The Archaeology of Knowledge.* Translated by A. M. Sheridan Smith. New York: Harper and Row, 1972.

———. *Foucault Live: Interviews, 1966–84.* Translated by John Johnston, edited by Sylvère Lotringer. New York: Semiotext(e), 1989.

———. *The Order of Things: An Archaeology of the Human Sciences.* New York: Vintage, 1994.

Freud, Sigmund. " 'A Child Is Being Beaten': A Contribution to the Study of the Origin of Sexual Perversions." In *The Standard Edition of the Complete Psychological Works of Sigmund Freud*. Translated by James Strachey et al., 17:175–203. London: The Hogarth Press, 1995.

———. *"Constructions in Analysis."* In *The Standard Edition of the Complete Psychological Works of Sigmund Freud*. Translated by James Strachey et al., 23:255–70. London: The Hogarth Press, 1995.

———. "Creative Writers and Day-Dreaming." In *The Standard Edition of the Complete Psychological Works of Sigmund Freud*. Translated by James Strachey et al., 9:141–54. London: The Hogarth Press, 1995.

———. "Mourning and Melancholia." In *The Standard Edition of the Complete Psychological Works of Sigmund Freud*. Translated by James Strachey et al., 14:243–58. London: The Hogarth Press, 1995.

Gaspard, Françoise. "Les Femmes dans les relations internationales." *Politique Étrangère* 3, no. 4 (2000): 731–41.

Gearhart, Suzanne. "Reply to Stephen Greenblatt." *New Literary History* 28, no. 3 (1997): 483–85.

———. "The Taming of Foucault: New Historicism, Psychoanalysis and the Subversion of Power." *New Literary History* 28, no. 3 (1997): 457–80.

Geertz, Clifford. "The World in Pieces: Culture and Politics at the End of the Century." In Clifford Geertz, *Available Light: Anthropological Reflections on Philosophical Topics*, 218–63. Princeton: Princeton University Press, 2000.

Göle, Nilüfer. *Interpénétrations: L'Islam et l'Europe*. Paris: Galaade, 2005.

Gordon, Lewis, T. D. Sharpley-Whiting, and Renée White, eds. *Fanon: A Critical Reader*. Cambridge, Mass.: Wiley-Blackwell, 1996.

De Gouges, Olympe de. *Déclaration des droits de la femme et de la citoyenne*. Paris, 1791.

Grewal, Inderpal. *Transnational America: Feminisms, Diasporas, Neoliberalisms*. Durham: Duke University Press, 2005.

Grogan, Susan K. *French Socialism and Sexual Difference: Women and the New Society, 1803–44*. London: Macmillan, 1992.

Gullickson, Gay. *Unruly Women of Paris: Images of the Commune*. Ithaca: Cornell University Press, 1996.

Gutting, G., ed. *The Cambridge Companion to Foucault*. Cambridge: Cambridge University Press, 1994.

Gutwirth, Madelyn. *The Twilight of the Goddesses: Women and Representation in the French Revolutionary Era*. New Brunswick, N.J.: Rutgers University Press, 1992.

Habib, Claude. *Consentement Amoureux*. Paris: Hachette, 1998.

———. *Galanterie française*. Paris: Gallimard, 2006.

Haraway, Donna J. *Simians, Cyborgs, and Women: The Reinvention of Nature*. New York: Routledge, 1991.

Higginbotham, Evelyn Brooks. "African-American Women's History and the

Metalanguage of Race." In *Feminism and History*, edited by Joan Wallach Scott, 183–208. Oxford: Oxford University Press, 1996.

Hobsbawm, Eric J., and Terence O. Ranger, eds. *The Invention of Tradition*. Cambridge: Cambridge University Press, 1983.

Hollander, John. *The Figure of Echo: A Mode of Allusion in Milton and After*. Berkeley: University of California Press, 1981.

Homer, Sean. "The Frankfurt School, the Father and the Social Fantasy." *New Formations* 38 (Summer 1999): 78–90.

Hunt, Lynn. *The Family Romance of the French Revolution*. Berkeley: University of California Press, 1992.

Huntington, Samuel P. *The Clash of Civilizations and the Remaking of World Order*. New York: Simon and Schuster, 1996.

Irigaray, Luce. "The Bodily Encounter with the Mother." In *The Irigaray Reader*, translated by David Macy and edited by Margaret Whitford, 34–46. Oxford: Blackwell, 1991.

Jakobsen, Janet R., and Ann Pellegrini. *Love the Sin: Sexual Regulation and the Limits of Religious Tolerance*. New York: New York University Press, 2003.

———, eds. *Secularisms*. Durham: Duke University Press, 2008.

Jardine, Alice, and Paul Smith, eds. *Men in Feminism*. New York: Methuen, 1987.

Kastoryano, Riva. "Religion and Incorporation: Islam in France." Unpublished paper presented at the Annual Meeting of the International Studies Association, New York, February 2009.

Keates, Debra. "Sexual Difference." In *Feminism and Psychoanalysis: A Critical Dictionary*, edited by Elizabeth Wright, 402–5. Oxford: Basil Blackwell, 1992.

Khanna, Ranjana. *Dark Continents: Psychoanalysis and Colonialism*. Durham: Duke University Press, 2003.

Knott, Sarah, and Barbara Taylor, eds. *Women, Gender, and Enlightenment*. Hampshire: Palgrave Macmillan, 2005.

Kristeva, Julia. "Stabat Mater." In *The Kristeva Reader*, edited by Toril Moi and translated by Leon S. Roudiez, 160–86. New York: Columbia University Press, 1986.

Lacan, Jacques. "Desire and the Interpretation of Desire in Hamlet." *Yale French Studies* no. 55–56 (1977).

———. *The Ethics of Psychoanalysis, 1959–1960*. Translated by Dennis Porter. New York: W. W. Norton, 1992.

———. *The Four Fundamental Concepts of Psycho-Analysis*. New York: W. W. Norton, 1981.

———. *On Feminine Sexuality: The Limits of Love and Knowledge*. Translated by Bruce Fink. New York: W. W. Norton, 1998.

———. "The Signification of the Phallus." In Jacques Lacan, *Ecrits*, translated by Alan Sheridan, 281–91. New York: W. W. Norton, 1977.

———. "Subversion of the Subject and the Dialectic of Desire in the Freudian Unconscious." In Jacques Lacan, *Ecrits*, translated by Alan Sheridan, 292–324. New York: W. W. Norton, 1977.

Laclos, Choderlos de. *Les liaisons dangereuses*. Translated by Douglas Parmée. Oxford: Oxford University Press, 2008.

Lairtullier, E. *Les femmes célèbres de 1789 à 1795, et leur influence dans la révolution, pour servir de suite et de complément à toutes les histoires de la révolution française*. 2 vols. Paris, 1840.

Langer, William L. "The Next Assignment." *American Historical Review* 63, no. 2 (1958): 283–304.

Laplanche, Jean. *Life and Death in Psychoanalysis*. Baltimore: Johns Hopkins University Press, 1976.

———. *New Foundations for Psychoanalysis*. Translated by David Macey. London: Basil Blackwell, 1989.

Laplanche, Jean, and Jean-Bertrand Pontalis. "Fantasy and the Origins of Sexuality." In *Formations of Fantasy*, edited by Victor Burgin, James Donald, and Cora Kaplan, 5–34. London: Routledge, 1986.

———. *The Language of Psycho-analysis*. Translated by Donald Nicholson-Smith. New York: W. W. Norton, 1974.

Laqueur, Thomas. *Making Sex: Body and Gender from the Greeks to Freud*. Cambridge: Harvard University Press, 1990.

Lazreg, Marnia. *The Eloquence of Silence: Algerian Women in Question*. New York: Routledge, 1994.

Lepore, Jill. "The Iceman." *New Yorker*, January 25, 2010, 24–30.

Levy, Darlene, Harriet Applewhite, and Mary Johnson, eds. *Women in Revolutionary Paris, 1789–1795*. Urbana: University of Illinois Press, 1979.

Lewis, Bernard. "The Revolt of Islam." *New Yorker*, November 19, 2001.

Loewenberg, Peter. *Decoding the Past: The Psychohistorical Approach*. New York: Alfred Knopf, 1983.

———. *Fantasy and Reality in History*. New York: Oxford University Press, 1995.

Mack, Phyllis. "Religion, Feminism, and the Problem of Agency: Reflections on Eighteenth-Century Quakerism." In *Women, Gender, and Enlightenment*, edited by Sarah Knott and Barbara Taylor, 434–59. Hampshire: Palgrave Macmillan, 2005.

Mahmood, Saba. *Politics of Piety: The Islamic Revival and the Feminist Subject*. Princeton: Princeton University Press, 2005.

Majid, Anouar. "The Politics of Feminism in Islam." *Signs* 23, no. 2 (1998): 322–61.

Manuel, Frank. "The Use and Abuse of Psychoanalysis for History." *Daedalus* 100, no. 1 (1971): 187–213.

Mathews, Donald G., and Jane Sherron De Hart. *Sex, Gender, and the Politics of the ERA: A State and the Nation*. New York: Oxford University Press, 1990.

McGoldrick, Dominic. *Human Rights and Religion: The Islamic Debate in Europe*. Portland, Ore.: Hart, 2006.

Modleski, Tania. *Feminism without Women: Culture and Criticism in a Postfeminist Age*. New York: Routledge, 1991.

Moghadam, Valentine. *Globalizing Women: Transnational Feminist Networks*. Baltimore: Johns Hopkins University Press, 2005.

Mohanty, Chandra Talpade. *Feminism without Borders: Decolonizing Theory, Practicing Solidarity.* Durham: Duke University Press, 2003.

Morgan, Robin, ed. *Sisterhood Is Global: The International Women's Movement Anthology.* Compiled, edited, introduced, with a new preface by Robin Morgan. New York: Feminist Press, 1996.

Najmabadi, Afsaneh. "Gender and the Sexual Politics of Public Visibility in Iranian Modernity." In *Going Public: Feminism and the Shifting Boundaries of the Private Sphere,* edited by Joan Wallach Scott and Debra Keates, 43–68. Urbana: University of Illinois Press, 2004.

——. "Teaching and Research in Unavailable Intersections." *differences* 9, no. 3 (1997): 65–78.

——. *Women with Mustaches and Men without Beards: Gender and Sexual Anxieties of Iranian Modernity.* Berkeley: University of California Press, 2005.

Nikolchina, Miglena. *Matricide in Language: Writing Theory in Kristeva and Woolf.* New York: Other Press, 2004.

——. "The Seminar: *Mode d'emploi.*" *differences* 13, no. 1 (2002): 96–127.

——. "Translating Gender: The Bulgarian Case." In *The Making of European Women's Studies,* edited by Rosi Braidotti, 3:92–94. Utrecht, the Netherlands: ATHENA, 2001.

Nouvet, Claire. "An Impossible Response: The Disaster of Narcissus." *Yale French Studies* no. 79 (1991): 103–34.

Nussbaum, Martha. *Women and Human Development: The Capabilities Approach.* Cambridge: Cambridge University Press, 2001.

Ovid. *Metamorphoses.* Translated by Frank Justus Miller. Edited by G. P. Goold. Cambridge: Cambridge University Press, 1977.

Ozouf, Mona. *Les mots des femmes: essai sur la singularité française.* Paris: Gallimard, 1995.

Pargellis, Stanley, ed. *The Quest for Political Unity in World History.* Vol. 3, *Annual Report of the American Historical Association for the Year 1942.* Washington: US Government Printing Office, 1944.

Parker, Harold T. "Review Essay: A Methodological Gem." *Journal of Urban History* 2, no. 3 (1976): 373–76.

Pateman, Carole. *The Sexual Contract.* London: Polity, 1988.

Pelletier, Madeleine. *La femme en lutte pour ses droits.* Paris, 1908.

——. *La femme vierge.* Paris: Valentin Bresle, 1933.

Plato. *Phaedrus.* Translated by R. Hackforth. Cambridge: Cambridge University Press, 1952.

Raynaud, Philippe. "Les femmes et la civilité: aristocratie et passions révolutionnaires." *Le Débat,* November–December 1989, 180–85.

Readings, Bill. *The University in Ruins.* Cambridge: Harvard University Press, 1996.

Riley, Denise. *"Am I That Name?" Feminism and the Category of "Women" in History.* London: Macmillan, 1988.

———. *The Words of Selves: Identification, Solidarity, Irony*. Stanford: Stanford University Press, 2000.

Riot-Sarcey, Michèle. *La démocratie à l'épreuve des femmes: trois figures critiques du pouvoir, 1830–1848*. Paris: Albin Michel, 1994.

Rivière, Joan. "Womanliness as a Masquerade." *International Journal of Psychoanalysis* 8 (1927): 303–13.

Rooney, Ellen, ed. *The Cambridge Companion to Feminist Literary Theory*. Cambridge: Cambridge University Press, 2006.

———. "Discipline and Vanish: Feminism, the Resistance to Theory, and the Politics of Cultural Studies." *differences* 2, no. 3 (1990): 14–28.

Rose, Jacqueline. *States of Fantasy*. Oxford: Oxford University Press, 1996.

Rosenvallon, Pierre. *Le modèle politique français: la société civile contre le jacobinisme de 1789 à nos jours*. Paris: Seuil, 2004.

Rubin, Gayle. "The Traffic in Women: Notes on the 'Political Economy' of Sex." In *Toward an Anthropology of Women*, edited by Rayna R. Reiter, 157–210. New York: Monthly Review Press, 1975.

Rupp, Leila. *Worlds of Women: The Making of an International Women's Movement*. Princeton: Princeton University Press, 1997.

Salecl, Renata. *The Spoils of Freedom: Psychoanalysis and Feminism after the Fall of Socialism*. London: Routledge, 1994.

Sands, Kathleen. "Feminisms and Secularisms." In *Secularisms*, edited by Janet R. Jakobsen and Ann Pellegrini, 308–29. Durham: Duke University Press, 2008.

Scott, Anne Firor, Sara M. Evans, Susan K. Cahn, and Elizabeth Faue. "Women's History in the New Millennium: A Conversation across Three Generations; Part I." *Journal of Women's History* 11, no. 1 (1999): 9–30.

———. "Women's History in the New Millennium: A Conversation across Three Generations; Part II." *Journal of Women's History* 11, no. 2 (1999): 199–220.

Scott, Joan Wallach. "Fantasy Echo: History and the Construction of Identity." *Critical Inquiry* 27 (Winter 2001).

———. *Feminism and History*, Oxford Readings in Feminism. Oxford: Oxford University Press, 1996.

———. "Finding Critical History." In *Becoming Historians*, edited by James Banner and John Gillis, 26–53. Chicago: University of Chicago Press, 2009.

———. "Gender: A Useful Category of Historical Analysis." *American Historical Review* 91, no. 5 (1986): 1053–75.

———. *Gender and the Politics of History*. New York: Columbia University Press, 1988.

———. *The Glassworkers of Carmaux: French Craftsmen and Political Action in a Nineteenth-Century City*. Cambridge: Harvard University Press, 1974.

———. "Multiculturalism and the Politics of Identity." In *The Identity in Question*, edited by John Rajchman, 3–12. New York: Routledge, 1995.

———. *Only Paradoxes to Offer: French Feminists and the Rights of Man*. Cambridge: Harvard University Press, 1996.

——. *Parité: Sexual Equality and the Crisis of French Universalism.* Chicago: University of Chicago Press, 2005.

——. *The Politics of the Veil.* Princeton: Princeton University Press, 2007.

——, ed. *Women's Studies on the Edge.* Durham: Duke University Press, 2009.

Scott, Joan Wallach, Cora Kaplan, and Debra Keates, eds. *Transitions, Environments, Translations: Feminism in International Politics.* New York: Routledge, 1997.

Scott, Joan Wallach, and Debra Keates, eds. *Going Public: Feminism and the Shifting Boundaries of the Private Sphere.* Bloomington: Indiana University Press, 2005.

Segal, Naomi. "Echo and Narcissus." In *Between Feminism and Psychoanalysis,* edited by Teresa Brennan, 168–85. New York: Routledge, 1989.

Serrière, Michèle. "Jeanne Deroin." In *Femmes et travail.* Paris: Matinsart, 1981.

Shepard, Todd. *The Invention of Decolonization: The Algerian War and the Remaking of France.* Ithaca: Cornell University Press, 2006.

Shepherdson, Charles. *Vital Signs: Nature, Culture, and Psychoanalysis.* New York: Routledge, 2000.

Silverstein, Paul. *Algeria in France: Transpolitics, Race, and Nation.* Bloomington: Indiana University Press, 2004.

Slama, Béatrice. "Écrits de femmes pendant la révolution." In *Les femmes et la révolution française: actes du colloque international, 12–13–14 avril 1989,* 2 vols., edited by Marie-France Brive, 2:291–306. Toulouse, France: Presses universitaires du Mirail, 1989.

Smith-Rosenberg, Carroll. "The Female World of Love and Ritual: Relations between Women in Nineteenth-Century America." *Signs* 1, no. 1 (1975): 1–29.

Snitow, Ann. "A Gender Diary." In *Conflicts in Feminism,* edited by Marianne Hirsch and Evelyn Fox Keller, 9–43. London: Routledge, 1990.

Snitow, Ann, Christine Stansell, and Sharon Thompson, eds. *The Powers of Desire: The Politics of Sexuality.* New York: Monthly Review Press, 1983.

Souffrant, Eddy. "To Conquer the Veil: Woman as a Critique of Liberalism." In *Fanon: A Critical Reader,* edited by Lewis Gordon, T. D. Sharpley-Whiting, and Renée White, 170–78. Cambridge, Mass.: Wiley-Blackwell, 1996.

Steedman, Carolyn. *Dust: The Archive and Cultural History.* New Brunswick, N.J.: Rutgers University Press, 2002.

Stites, Richard. *The Women's Liberation Movement in Russia: Feminism, Nihilism, and Bolshevism, 1860–1930.* Princeton: Princeton University Press, 1978.

Surkis, Judith. "Carnival Balls and Penal Codes: Body Politics in July Monarchy France." *History of the Present* 1, no. 1 (2011): 59–83.

Taylor, Charles. *A Secular Age.* Cambridge: Harvard University Press, 2007.

Tešanović, Jasmina. *Me and My Multicultural Street.* Belgrade, Serbia: Feministicka, 2001.

Tocqueville, Alexis de. *Souvenirs.* Paris: Gallimard, 1964.

Tsing, Anna Lowenhaupt. "Transitions as Translations." In *Transitions, Environ-*

ments, Translations: Feminism in International Politics, edited by Joan Wallach Scott, Cora Kaplan, and Debra Keates, 253–72. New York: Routledge, 1997.

Vance, Carole S., ed. *Pleasure and Danger*. New York: Routledge, 1984.

Viennot, Eliane, ed. *La démocratie à la française ou les femmes indésirables*. Paris: Cahiers du CEDREF, 2002.

———. *La France, les femmes, et le pouvoir*. 2 vols. Paris: Perrin, 2006 and 2008.

Walton, Jean. *Fair Sex, Savage Dreams: Race, Psychoanalysis, Sexual Difference*. Durham: Duke University Press, 2001.

Weed, Elizabeth. "Feminist Psychoanalytic Literary Criticism." In *The Cambridge Companion to Feminist Literary Theory*, edited by Ellen Rooney, 261–80. Cambridge: Cambridge University Press, 2006.

———. "Gender and Sexual Difference in Joan W. Scott: From the 'Useful' to the 'Impossible.'" In *The Question of Gender: Engaging with Joan W. Scott's Critical Feminism*, edited by Judith Butler and Elizabeth Weed. Bloomington: Indiana University Press, 2012.

Whitford, Margaret, ed. *The Irigaray Reader*. Oxford: Blackwell Publishers, 1991.

Wiegman, Robyn. "Feminism, Institutionalism, and the Idiom of Failure." *differences* 11, no. 3 (1999–2000): 107–36.

———. "What Ails Feminist Criticism? A Second Opinion." *Critical Inquiry* 25, no. 2 (1999): 362–79.

Wilson, Kathleen. *The Island Race: Englishness, Empire, and Gender in the Eighteenth Century*. London: Routledge, 2003.

Wright, Elizabeth, ed. *Feminism and Psychoanalysis: A Critical Dictionary*. Oxford: Basil Blackwell, 1992.

Young, Iris Marion. "The Logics of Masculinist Protection: Reflections on the Current Security State." *Signs* 29, no. 1 (2003): 1–25.

Zimmerman, Andrew. *Alabama in Africa: Booker T. Washington, the German Empire and the Globalization of the New South*. Princeton: Princeton University Press, 2010.

Žižek, Slavoj. *The Plague of Fantasies*. London: Verso, 1997.

———. *The Sublime Object of Ideology*. London: Verso, 1989.

Index

JOAN WALLACH SCOTT
is the Harold F. Linder Professor
of Social Science at the Institute
for Advanced Study.

Library of Congress Cataloging-in-Publication Data
Scott, Joan Wallach.
The fantasy of feminist history / Joan Wallach Scott.
p. cm.—(Next wave provocations)
Includes bibliographical references and index.
ISBN 978-0-8223-5113-9 (cloth : alk. paper)
ISBN 978-0-8223-5125-2 (pbk. : alk. paper)
1. Feminism—History. 2. Psychoanalysis and feminism.
3. Feminist theory. I. Title. II. Series: Next wave provocations.
HQ1122.S36 2012
305.4201—dc23   2011021965